THE HEART
OF A
CHAMPION

D1113165

THE HEART OF A CHAMPION

Edited by
Thomas and Sheila Jones

DPI
DISCIPLESHIP
PUBLICATIONS
INTERNATIONAL

One Merrill Street
Woburn, MA 01801
1-800-727-8273
Fax: (617) 937-3889

The Heart of a Champion
©1996 by Discipleship Publications International
One Merrill Street, Woburn, MA 01801

Printed in the United States of America

Cover design: Chris Costello
Interior design: Chris Costello and Laura Root

ISBN 1-884553-93-1

Acknowledgments

Our thanks to the following people who contributed in various ways to this project. Without their willing hearts and generous help, the result you see here would not have been possible.

Janet Appleby
Phil Arsenault
Carl Christensen
Chris Costello
Fred Faller
Tom Foote
Kim Hanson
Jerry Hixon
Scott Leete
Amby Murphy

Jerri Newman
Janet O'Donnell
David Rosa
Tom Scotto
Carla Scotto
Mike Smart
Steve Staten
Larry Wood
Lea Wood
Steve Zedler

CONTENTS

Week One: PREPARATION

Week Two: PEOPLE

Week Three: PASSION

Week Four: PERSEVERANCE

INTRODUCTION

STIRRING THE HEART WITH A NOBLE THEME

"My heart is stirred by a noble theme," wrote one of the Psalmists of Israel (Psalm 45:1). There are few human events that are more stirring than the Olympic Games. The courage, the determination, the sacrifice, the commitment we see in many athletes moves us, sometimes even to tears. With this book, built around the theme of the Games and the lives of those who have left lasting impressions, our goal is to stir the hearts of disciples of Jesus Christ around the world. As this book goes to press, athletes from all over the globe are preparing to journey to Atlanta for the centennial edition of the modern Olympic Games. For a hundred years now, modern Olympic athletes have been showing qualities to the world that are not only inspiring, but worthy of imitation.

Athletic competition and the Olympics in particular were well known to the early Christian writers. Having begun in Greece in 393 B.C., the ancient Olympic Games were still popular in New Testament times, continuing until the fourth century A.D. The qualities that made for great athletic endeavors did not go unnoticed by the biblical writers. Paul and others saw the Christian life as a great race, requiring disciples to apply to the spiritual realm many of the vital qualities that made one an athletic champion.

In writing to the Corinthian disciples, who lived not far from Mount Olympus and had surely grown up hearing story after story of the athletes who competed there, Paul made his most detailed reference to the games and the competition:

Do you not know that in a race all the runners run,
but only one gets the prize? Run in such a way as to

*get the prize. Everyone who competes in the games
goes into strict training. They do it to get a crown
that will not last; but we do it to get a crown that
will last forever. Therefore I do not run like a man
running aimlessly; I do not fight like a man beating
the air. No, I beat my body and make it my slave so
that after I have preached to others, I myself will
not be disqualified for the prize.*

1 CORINTHIANS 9:24-27

Paul's statement makes two things very clear: (1) *Disciples
can learn important principles from those who compete in the
games.* It is well worth our time to look at them and what
causes them to excel. (2) *What disciples do with these principles is far more important than what the athletes do.* In Paul's
day they did it to get a crown of laurel that would not last. In
our day they do it for a gold medal, maybe an endorsement
contract, or a moment of glory, but these also will not last.
On the other hand, when disciples focus on their mission,
when they train hard, when they push through the pain,
when they overcome the obstacles, when they compete according to the rules, and never, *never* give up, they get re-
sults that last forever and ever. You may never enter the Olympic arena. You may not get the gold or the silver or the bronze.
But if you join Jesus' team, pour your heart out for his cause
and stay in the race until you reach the finish line, you will
have something more valuable than gold (1 Peter 1:7).

In each devotional reading in this book, you will be introduced to someone who made their mark in the Olympic
Games or in another well-known athletic event. The goal is
to learn from them and respond to biblical challenges with
the same heart and spirit. If you have children, get the com-
panion volume for kids and enjoy an inspiring month together with great talks every day. Above all, as you read and
as you think, pray for the heart of a champion. With the
power of God, we can all be winners!

Week One

PREPARATION

THE RACE MARKED OUT FOR US

**Spiridon Louis
· MARATHON ·
Greece**

In 490 B.C. with only 7,000 troops the Greeks defeated 20,000 Persian invaders in the celebrated Battle of Marathon. Following the great victory, the Greek commander sent out a lone runner from the battle site to Athens, to deliver the good news (as in Isaiah 52:7). When the runner reached Athens, approximately 26 miles away, he cried, "Rejoice, we conquer!" then dropped dead on the spot.

When the Olympic Games were revived after a 1,400 year hiatus, the organizers decided to include a race from Marathon to Athens, and thus the grueling event known around the world today was born. In that first marathon 18 competitors, 12 of them from Greece, looked ahead to a race none of them had any experience in running.

The marathon was the final event of the competition, as it still is today, and began with an anxious Greek crowd of 70,000 seated in the Olympic stadium. Even with their athletic tradition and the presence of the most competitors of any country, the Greeks had not won a single event in track and field. The Greek press called for an end to the farce.

The progress of the race was reported back to the crowd via men on horseback and bicycles. At times the crowd was visibly depressed as the lead changed back and forth between athletes from France and Austria. Finally, the first of the runners approached the gates of the stadium for the dramatic finish. Once the crowd realized who he was, the noise was deafening. *"Hellas! Hellas!"* ("A Greek! A Greek!") they shouted. The two princes of Greece, George and Constantine, jumped from their royal box and accompanied Spiridon Louis to the finish line. A humble shepherd, he had trained for the event by running alongside his horse as he delivered water to those in the countryside.

Spiridon was offered many prizes for his Olympic win including a sewing machine, free haircuts, and even a wife—but he refused all of these. He finally accepted a horse and cart because he said he needed them to carry water back home. His attitude was, "I have only done my duty." He sought no fame or fortune for himself.

Since that fateful day in 1896, hundreds of thousands of runners have crossed the finish lines in marathon events all around the world. A humble shepherd led the way, and many have followed.

Therefore, since we are surrounded by such a great cloud of witnesses, let us throw off everything that hinders and the sin that so easily entangles, and let us run with perseverance the race marked out for us.
HEBREWS 12:1-2

The running of the marathon is a very fitting way to begin this book. At least seven times in the New Testament the Christian life is compared to a race. For most of us this race will not be a sprint. It will not even be a middle-distance race. It will be a marathon. We will run to the tops of hills, and we will run down into valleys. Sometimes the road will be smooth, sometimes very rough. The race marked out for us is one that will require training, great endurance and a serious commitment to go the distance. We may never have undertaken anything like it before. Like Spiridon Louis, we may seem unlikely candidates for such an endeavor. But there is only one issue that is important: *This is the race God has marked out for us.* It may be a challenge. It may bring pain. There may be times when we wonder if we can go on. But this race is not optional. It is not just for the spiritually elite. It is for the ordinary shepherds of this world.

As we run the race, we must see and hear, with the eyes and ears of faith, the great crowd of witnesses cheering us on. We must feel the support of all the saints who have gone before us and all our brothers and sisters who are now in our lives. We must hear the crowd chanting, *"Christianos! Christianos!"* ("A Christian! A Christian!"). We must look forward to having the Son of God jump from the royal box and accompany us across the finish line. The principles we will study in this book will challenge us and stretch us, but we must keep in mind the great joy of the victory that will be ours.

Spiridon is remembered in Olympic history for his humility. While this cannot be said of every great star of the Games, it is the one quality that is most essential for us, as Christians, as we seek to run the race marked out for us. We must not be in the race for our glory, but for the glory of God. We must be confident not in our own ability, but in God's power. We must not think the victory comes from looking within but from fixing our eyes on Jesus.

INTO YOUR LIFE

1. Why did you decide to run the race the Bible says is marked out for us?

2. What is the impact on athletes of a crowd of fans cheering and applauding? What can you do to hear more clearly the cheers of those in the "Kingdom Stadium"?

3. What action can you take when you begin to think that the race is too hard or too long?

4. Do you desire humility? Do you pray for it? Do you ask others to help you with it? How does it show up in your life? Why is it such a key to successfully running the Christian race?

THE POWER OF TRAINING

Vladimir Sainikov
· SWIMMING ·
Soviet Union (Russia)

None of the athletes you are reading about in this book would have made their mark without dedication to strict training. Talent means a great deal, but without training it all goes to waste. Even those with lesser talent can become champions when they have great heart and a commitment to training. While there are legions of examples of athletes in strict training, Vladimir Sainikov of Russia is one of the most outstanding.

As a child he was skinny and often sick with colds and ear infections, but coach Igor Koshkin saw in him a man who could become a great long-distance swimmer. Koshkin laid out the demands and Sainikov responded. His daily routine involved six 500-meter swims before breakfast, an hour of lifting weights in the afternoon, and six more 500-meter swims before the evening meal. Although nagged by ear infections, he remained steadfast in his training. He eventually lengthened his daily swims to a total of 20 kilometers.

The more he trained, the more his times improved. In 1976 in Montreal he was the first Soviet team member to reach the finals in the 1500 meters and eventually finished fifth behind the American Brian Goodell. In 1980 with the Americans boycotting the Games in Moscow, he was competing mainly against the clock, setting a new world record in the 400 meters and becoming the first man ever to break the 15-minute mark in the 1500 meters.

In 1984 it was the Soviets' turn to boycott, and Sainikov was denied the opportunity to compete in Los Angeles. However, in 1986 at the Goodwill Games he did win the gold against the U.S., setting a world record in the 800-meter freestyle.

The following year his times fell off badly and many thought his career was over. But he had not forgotten those training habits learned early, and incredibly he was back at the Olympics in Seoul in 1988. He was 28 years old, at the age when most swimmers have long since retired. If he was to win a gold medal, he would have to become the oldest swimmer to do so in 48 years. The skeptics abounded, but he outswam all his younger competitors in the grueling 1500 meters and brought another gold medal back to Leningrad.

Without the tremendous dedication to training developed early in his career Sainikov would have never become the swimming legend he is.

Everyone who competes in the games goes into strict training. They do it to get a crown that will not last; but we do it to get a crown that will last forever.
1 CORINTHIANS 9:25

Strict training: "*They* do it," says Paul. Athletes do it. The Vladimir Sainikovs of the world do it. Strict training: "*we* do it," says Paul. The Pauls and Timothys, the Priscillas and the Aquilas of the kingdom of God do it. Disciples do it. Paul takes it for granted that disciples will have their own routines, their own regimens, their own plans to develop and increase their effectiveness. He even assumes we will be more committed to such things because we have a higher motivation and a greater goal.

Athletes know better than to change into their shorts and run onto the track without training. They know what humiliation would await them. But do we as disciples try to take on the greatest challenge ever offered to men and women without training? Do we often go up against a powerful and cunning opponent without having dedicated ourselves to being prepared and equipped? Is it any wonder that some experience defeat?

Paul says, "but we do it." But do we? What training have you received since becoming a disciple? What training habits did you develop early in your Christian life? How committed have you remained to those? What things do you daily? What things do you do weekly? Is there any reason to think that your spiritual life will be successful, making a difference in the lives of others, if you just show up and hope it happens?

"Train yourself to be godly. For physical training is of some value, but godliness has value for all things, holding promise for both the present life and the life to come" (1 Timothy 4:7-8). Hours in the pool and hours in the weight room helped make Vladimir a champion. That had some value, but when we train to be godly we do something that has value for all things impacting not only this life but the life to come. Time spent in Bible study, prayer, discipling times and reading powerful Christian books will not be without effect.

The Bible says training needs to begin as early as possible. Christian parents—specifically fathers—are told "... do not exasperate your children; instead, bring them up in the *training* and instruction of the Lord" (Ephesians 6:4, emphasis added). At an early age children need to be memorizing scriptures and learning to have quiet times during which they learn and grow as children of God. But, as Vladimir learned, training is also important for those who have been around, even a long time. If we want to go on to greater things for God, our training must never end.

Into Your Life

1. How have you seen the power of training in your life or in the lives of some you know well?

2. What is your attitude toward training? Can anyone be a powerful disciple if they resist training? If your attitude has not been so great, where do you think you need to look to find the source of the problem?

3. List the major elements in your current spiritual training program. Talk through these with someone. What do you need to change?

4. A question for leaders: What are you doing to set your people up for success in this area? What training are you giving them? Is it one-dimensional, or does it give them help and direction in a number of areas?

WEAKNESS TURNED TO STRENGTH

Wilma Rudolph
· TRACK AND FIELD ·
United States

Born two months premature at four-and-a-half pounds, Wilma Rudolph was a fragile child. By the time she was four, she had contracted mumps, measles, chicken pox, scarlet fever, double pneumonia and crippling polio. Doctors did not expect her to walk again without a brace, but Wilma's mother refused to accept such limitations. Twice a week for years, she took Wilma for physical therapy, traveling by bus to the black hospital in Nashville fifty miles away. Every night, family members would take turns stretching and massaging her leg.

Sidelined for years with her metal-and-leather brace, Wilma would spend hours observing the other children's games, imagining how she would avoid their mistakes. Slowly, her leg grew stronger, and she wore the brace less and less. By age twelve, she was able to walk without it.

But Wilma did more than walk. The once crippled girl became a teenager known for her grace and speed. She attracted the attention of Ed Temple, the track coach at Tennessee State University. Working over the summer with his college track team, Wilma benefited enormously from two things: her own dedication to training and his outstanding coaching. Along with her mentor from TSU, Mae Faggs, veteran of two Olympics, Wilma qualified for the 1956 Olympic team and competed in the Games in Melbourne while still a high-school student. She failed to qualify for the finals in one event but ran with the relay team for a bronze medal. Disappointed, she vowed to return and do better.

After completing her senior year in high school, Wilma entered TSU on a track scholarship. Four years and hours and hours of training later, she had matured as an athlete under Coach Temple and had set American and world records in her events. At the Olympic trials, six members of the TSU women's track team qualified, and Ed Temple was chosen to be the Olympic coach.

The day of her first race, Wilma fought off the "distraction" of a sprained ankle and still won a gold medal. It was the first of the three golds she would bring home from the Rome Olympic Games in 1960. Throughout the Games, her speed brought her across the finish line, and her grace brought her international acclaim, but she probably would not have been there at all without family, coaches and teammates who had encouraged her over the years.

And what more shall I say? I do not have time to tell about Gideon, Barak, Samson, Jephthah, David, Samuel and the prophets, who through faith conquered kingdoms, administered justice, and gained what was promised; who shut the mouths of lions, quenched the fury of the flames, and escaped the edge of the sword; whose weakness was turned to strength; and who became powerful in battle and routed foreign armies.

HEBREWS 11:32-34

If Ms. Rudolph's neighbors had been told that her crippled child would become one of the most famous athletes in Olympic history, they would have shook their heads in understandable disbelief. When we see weakness, we have a very difficult time imagining how it can become strength. But if it can happen in the physical realm, how much more can it happen in the spiritual realm?

Many biblical heroes hardly looked the part when they were first called. Our theme passage today mentions Gideon. In his own words, his clan was the weakest in his tribe, and more than that, he was the least in his family (Judges 6:15). Talk about lower than low! But God turned his weakness to strength, and with the power of God he defeated an army many times larger with only 300 men.

Jeremiah heard God's call for him to be a prophet and said, "I'm only a child" (Jeremiah 1:6). He didn't exactly sound like a champion. Ezekiel received visions showing him what God wanted from his life. Then he looked at the obstacles that lay before him and sat beside the Kebar River for seven days "overwhelmed" (Ezekiel 3:15). A future hall-of-famer? He didn't look like one.

Peter, when Jesus first called him, and for long time after that, hardly appeared to be the "Rock" Jesus believed he could become.

Even Moses doubted God's choice. Having left Egypt in disgrace and fear, (Exodus 2:11-15), he was chosen by God to lead Israel out of slavery. *Surely a mistake has been made.* Moses' excuses flowed like a river—even to the point of testing God's patience. Wrapped up in insecurity, Moses did not believe he had what it would take. The truth is, we are all weak when we are called. No one has what it takes for spiritual victory without the transforming touch of God.

The Wilma Rudolph of the 1960 Olympic Games was a totally different person from the feeble child of the 1930s. A mother who wouldn't give up, family members who sacrificed, eventually a coach who knew what was best, combined with her own willingness to go into strict training made all the difference. Why are we so sure that our weaknesses cannot be turned into strengths? Our own determination to grow combined with a God who has all power and a loving spiritual family where we will get support and direction can result in a miracle make-over.

The Bible says God is very much like Wilma's mother. He will "take you to Nashville" or *wherever* you need to go. He'll bring others into your life to strengthen and encourage you, and he won't stop believing that you can run and that you can win.

INTO YOUR LIFE

1. What are your weaknesses? Do they hold you back? Do you nurse them, or cry out to God to make them become strengths? Have you prayed with faith? Do you continue praying?

2. Do you primarily see the weaknesses or the strengths of others? Don't answer too quickly. How do you communicate your vision for your brothers and sisters? How do you think this affects them?

3. When struggling with your circumstances, how would allowing others into your life help you to stay in the battle? How often do you pray with others about your struggles?

4. What is something God probably believes you can do that you have not yet accepted? Pray for the courage to surrender to God's dreams for you.

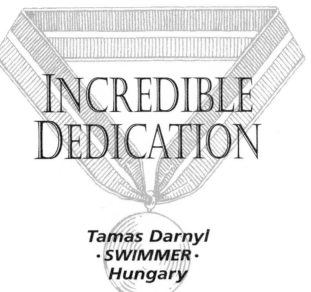

INCREDIBLE DEDICATION

Tamas Darnyl
·SWIMMER·
Hungary

In 1984, Tamas Darnyl had reached his goal of joining the great Hungarian swim team, but because of the Eastern Bloc boycott of the L.A. Games he stayed home in Budapest with a heavy heart. But four years later at the Seoul Olympics, he finally got his chance. Tamas had done his homework. He knew his opponents well and plotted a race strategy which consisted of times of restraint and times of just all-out pushing. His work paid off—in gold! He won two medals in the 200-meter and 400-meter individual medleys setting new world records. He returned to Barcelona in 1992 to do something never done before: win gold medals in those same two events in back-to-back Olympics.

What made Hungarian swimmer Tamas Darnyl an Olympic champion? It wasn't his size. In the pool, where winners hit the wall only tenths of an inch apart, height can be of great advantage. Yet Tamas was only 6'1", and his strongest competitors, like Michael Gross and Matt Biondi, were 6'6". It certainly wasn't a perfect "swimmer's physique." He didn't have it. In Budapest, Hungary, where swimmers are as numerous as basketball players are in the U.S., there was nothing physically that distinguished him from any other contender—nothing that would have indicated his future greatness.

What really put Tamas in a class all by himself was his competitive spirit and his sharp mind. Once he decided to try out for the Olympic team, he trained vigorously. With the help of his father and later his coach, he pushed himself beyond what other swimmers were doing. His daily workout started at 6 a.m. and ended at 5 p.m. John Urbanchek, a native Hungarian and coach at the University of Michigan, put it plainly: "What Tamas lacks in natural talent, he makes up for with incredible dedication." What made Tamas a champion? *Incredible dedication.*

Tamas Darnyl proved again that while the condition of the body is important in athletics, the condition of the mind and the heart is even more important. Dedication. Devotion. Commitment. Consecration. Single-mindedness. These are the qualities of champions.

Were not the Cushites and Libyans a mighty army with great numbers of chariots and horsemen? Yet when you relied on the LORD, he delivered them into your hand. For the eyes of the LORD range throughout the earth to strengthen those whose hearts are fully committed to him.

2 CHRONICLES 16:8-9

The eyes of the Lord do not range throughout the earth to find those with the greatest minds or the greatest bodies. God does not draft like the NFL or the NBA, and he doesn't recruit like Harvard or Stanford. What God's radar is set to detect are hearts that are fully committed to him. When he finds those hearts, he strengthens them, he blesses them, he empowers them. He does his divine thing in their lives.

We can be lacking in many areas, but God is not bothered in the least. Maybe we don't have an imposing physical presence. Perhaps we do not have a booming or resonating voice that immediately commands attention. Our test scores through the years may not indicate a great mind. Our personality may not be charismatic. If these qualities are there, God wants to use them, for sure. But none of that really matters to God. He has one concern above all others: *Is his or her heart fully committed to me?*

The Bible could not be any plainer about this than it is in 1 Samuel 16:6-7:

> When they arrived, Samuel saw Eliab and thought, "Surely the LORD's anointed stands here before the LORD."
>
> But the LORD said to Samuel, "Do not consider his appearance or his height, for I have rejected him. The LORD does not look at the things man looks at. Man looks at the outward appearance, but the LORD looks at the heart."

As a result, David, who was not one of the more imposing candidates, was anointed to be king. God's radar had found what it was looking for: a committed heart.

Commitment. Dedication. Consecration. Devotion. All of these things take a lot out of you, but they give back ten-, twenty-, thirty-, a hundredfold. "Give, and it will be given to you," said Jesus. "A good measure, pressed down, shaken together and running over, will be poured into your lap. For with the measure you use, it will be measured to you" (Luke 6:38). Dedication always translates into giving—giving hours, sweat, patience, perseverance, prayers, counsel, tears. Those who are willing to give find that God is willing and ready to bless. Do you believe it? Do you believe with all your heart?

Tamas Darnyl's dedication cost him much but brought him not one, not two, not three, but four gold medals and a place in Olympic history. Make no mistake about it: Our dedication to Jesus Christ will cost us. Look at Jesus himself.

Look at Paul. Look at the early church. Some will say the price is too high. Many will look for an easier road. But remember Jesus' words: "And everyone who has left houses or brothers or sisters or father or mother or children or fields for my sake will receive a hundred times as much *and will inherit eternal life*" (Matthew 19:29-30, emphasis added). Costly dedication has its privileges and its rewards.

Dedication. Devotion. Commitment. Consecration. Single-mindedness. These are the qualities of Christians.

INTO YOUR LIFE

1. What is there about you that has caused you to think that God cannot use you powerfully? Is this something that you have been able to settle once and for all, or does it still nag at you from time to time? How does this chapter help you to get a godly perspective?

2. To what extent do the words *dedication, devotion, commitment, consecration, single-mindedness* describe your character? Don't be negative or down on yourself, but take a sober look.

3. What will be some of the specific costs of being committed and devoted? Do you pay the price gladly?

4. What one change can you make in order to have a more daily-dedicated character? Is it being consistent in your times with God? Is it eliminating a certain distraction? For you, specifically, what is it? Now go after it!

RESTORING THE GLORY

Lasse Viren
· DISTANCE RUNNER ·
Finland

From 1912 to 1936 middle-distance and long-distance runners from Finland won a remarkable 37 medals in six Olympiads in the men's events, with 21 of those being gold. The "Flying Finns" dominated these events in track and field like few teams ever have.

But then the glory departed. For the next 30 years the Finns were a shadow of their former selves. In 1965 16-year-old Lasse Viren listened to his radio and felt his heart sink as he heard the report of Finland losing to Sweden in the annual meet between the two countries. Feeling that his country should be ashamed of its performance, Viren vowed that one day he would change things.

Badly yearning for his country to regain past glory, he trained hard, developing his stamina by running in sandhills. In 1972 at the Munich Olympic Games he was ready to give his best. In the 10,000-meter run, almost half way through the race he found himself in a not-too-distant fifth place when what seemed to be disaster struck. Viren stumbled and fell as the others left him behind. Seemingly out of the race, Viren scrambled to his feet and refused to quit. Surely few observers would have given him much of a chance, but slowly he gained on the leaders. With 600 meters left he passed them all, eventually winning with a world record time of 27:38.4. A few days later he added a second gold medal as he won the 5,000-meter event in far less dramatic fashion. The Finns were flying again. His teenage dream had come true. No longer did his country need to be ashamed.

But to prove 1972 was no fluke, he was back again in Montreal in 1976 seeking to do what no runner had ever done before: win the 5,000 and 10,000 in two successive Olympiads. He made it look easy, winning the 10,000 by 30 meters and capturing the 5,000 without suspense. Viren had brought the glory back to Finland.

She named the boy Ichabod, saying, "The glory has departed from Israel"—because of the capture of the ark of God and the deaths of her father-in-law and her husband. She said, "The glory has departed from Israel, for the ark of God has been captured."
1 SAMUEL 4:21-22

After the crumbling of the kingdom of Israel, the people longed for the glory that was once theirs as a nation. The times of power and comfort and wealth were gone. When their enemies, the Philistines, captured the ark of God, the people mourned and despaired the loss of the very presence of God among them. The glory had departed from Israel. Those who cared knew this was not right and that things needed to change.

When Jesus came, it disturbed him greatly to see that those who were supposed to be the people of God no longer reflected the glory of God. To those selling and buying animals and exchanging money in the temple area, this protector of God's honor made a statement impossible to misunderstand, "How dare you turn my Father's house into a market!" (John 2:16) He lived out the Old Testament scripture, "Zeal for your house will consume me" (Psalm 69:9; John 2:17).

Today the church is the new Israel of God and the house of God, and disciples of Jesus must be zealous to see that the glory does not depart. We must remember the glory days of the first-century disciples and be committed to seeing the church today be just as zealous, just as sacrificial, just as loving, just as glorious for God as the church was at the beginning.

Just as Lasse Viren's heart sank as he heard of Finland's loss to her rival, so must our hearts sink anytime we hear of the church's defeats to Satan. Anytime we have a "God and me" mentality, we are missing the point of his people, his nation, his church. It is not just "God and me;" it is much more "God and we" (pardon the grammar). Our loyalty to his church should be fierce; our commitment must drive us to protect the loss of his honor; and our zeal should compel us to restore the loss of his glory.

Paul reminded the Philippians, "our citizenship is in heaven" (Philippians 3:20). Philippi was a colony of Rome, endowing its people with coveted Roman citizenship. We, the church, are a colony of heaven. Our true citizenship is in heaven itself, and we must represent heaven well.

Our hearts are certainly moved as we realize the tremendous sense of national pride exhibited by Viren and other Olympic athletes. We can appreciate their loyalty in desiring to maintain the glory of their respective countries. But how much more should we, as citizens of heaven itself, seek to maintain the glory of God's nation on this earth! As far as it lies within each of us, may the glory of God never depart from his church!

Into Your Life

1. How real is your loyalty to the church? Do you tend to view the church as an organization or as family? Does zeal for God's house consume you?

2. When are times when you think God is disappointed in his church and sad, or even angry, about what is going on?

3. How do you feel when you hear of a victory of Satan that hurts the church? Does your heart sink? Do you complain, or do you act? What action do you take?

4. What can you do to help restore and revive the glory in the church?

DETERMINATION THAT DEFEATS DISCOURAGEMENT

Lis Hartel
· EQUESTRIAN ·
Denmark

It was 1944. Lis Hartel, a 23-year-old equestrian, was pregnant when she received devastating news: She had polio, a feared crippler. As a result, this young woman with great ambitions was left almost entirely paralyzed. Who, in her shoes, would not have felt discouraged? But Lis Hartel was a determined woman. She refused to surrender to this cruel disease and began an intense physical therapy program. Slowly, through tedious training she began to regain use of her arms and, later, her legs.

Before the onset of her illness, Lis had competed in the equestrian event known as dressage, one in which the horse and rider perform various maneuvers with no oral command. The rider and horse must be united completely as points are lost for lack of symmetry. Dressage has its origins in military history as a sport only for the noble and the elite. The exercise was practiced by Napoleon's famous horsemen and imperial guard.

But in the 1940s, polio was not Lis' only problem. She dreamed of performing in the Olympics, but the Olympic committee had not opened dressage to female riders. In fact, only male *commissioned* officers were allowed to enter. However, as she worked to rehabilitate herself, times were changing. By 1952 the doors for women were opened, and Lis was ready.

Although still challenged by legs that did not work normally, she earned a place on the Danish equestrian team in both the 1952 and 1956 Olympics. She needed assistance to mount and dismount her horse, but once in the saddle, she competed with poise and grace. In a sport where fluency of motion is scrutinized, the weakness and jerky movements that often come with polio could have been detrimental. Yet, Lis performed in unison with her horse and won the silver medal. Four years later she repeated her amazing success taking another silver medal at the Melbourne Olympiad. Each time she had to humbly accept help onto the winners' platform, but she proved what a heart full of determination can do.

"This is the meaning of the parable: The seed is the word of God. Those along the path are the ones who hear, and then the devil comes and takes away the word from their hearts, so that they may not believe and be saved. Those on the rock are the ones who receive the word with joy when they hear it, but they have no root. They believe for a while, but in the time of testing they fall away. The seed that fell among thorns stands for those who hear, but as they go on their way they are choked by life's worries, riches and pleasures, and they do not mature. But the seed on good soil stands for those with a noble and good heart, who hear the word, retain it, and by persevering produce a crop.

LUKE 8:11-15

We get introduced to the real Jesus. We learn of his plan for our lives. We become his disciples and start dreaming about ways God can use us. But then "polio" strikes. It may be a health problem or a difficult marriage or a family situation. It may be unemployment or other financial challenges. Discouragement can come in many forms. Our spiritual enemy will find something that will hit us all.

During discouraging times we need great conviction that God's way is so right that we will be determined to stay with the goals, the plans and the dreams no matter what it may take. When Lis Hartel started her career as an equestrian, she had no idea she would have to deal with the added burden of polio. Competing at such a high level was challenging enough, and when the polio hit, it would have been easy to have said, "I hadn't counted on this. Guess that's it for this dream." But she was determined—determined to deal with the unexpected, and not allow the unexpected to become a deterrent.

As we take up the cross and follow Jesus, we will all get hit by some of those "unexpected things." They will test our hearts, test our resolve, and test our commitment. But if we have the good heart—the heart of a champion—we will not "fall away." We will retain that word we have heard from God, and we will persevere. Our goal will be more important than our problem. Our God will be bigger than the obstacle.

We may feel the hit. We may ask questions. We may do some agonizing. We may need some long sessions of crying out to God, but if we understand who Jesus is, we will go to spiritual rehab, and we will do whatever God says it takes to get back on that horse and ride for him.

INTO YOUR LIFE

1. What obstacles have you already encountered in your Christian life? How did you respond? What did you learn about responses to future obstacles?

2. What challenge can you think of that makes your heart sink and causes you to say, "I just couldn't handle that"? Look up scriptures that can change your attitude, and spend some time praying for more faith.

3. When bad things happen, what lies of Satan are you tempted to believe? How do you recognize and disarm those lies?

4. How does Romans 8:18 give perspective when times of difficulty come?

USING ALL YOUR TALENTS

Babe Didrikson Zaharias
· TRACK AND FIELD ·
United States

Mildrid "Babe" Didrikson was born on June 26, 1914, in Port Arthur, Texas. The daughter of Norwegian immigrant parents, she was nicknamed "Babe" after Babe Ruth because of her ability to hit home runs playing baseball. Believing strongly in athletic training for his children, her father set up a gym in the backyard.

Because of her natural ability and willingness to work hard, she was good at many sports. After getting help from the coach of the boys' basketball team in her high school, she made the girls' team and became their best scorer. Later, she helped her amateur team win the national title and scored an amazing 108 points in one game! Colonel McDubbs, sponsor of the team, formed a track and field team, and Babe excelled in not just two or three, not just five or six, but in *all ten* of the featured events.

In the AAU championships which also doubled as the Olympic trials of 1932, she *was* the team, a lone star of Texas if you will. She placed first in 5 events, tied for first in a 6th, finished second in a 7th, and placed in all the remaining events but one. Amazingly, she went from event to event in a two-and-a-half hour period. Texas (actually Babe!) won the overall competition and Babe went to the 1932 Olympics held in Los Angeles.

The Olympic rules prevented her from competing in any more than three events. She won the gold in the javelin, setting a new Olympic and world record. She won the gold in the 80-meter hurdles, again setting a new Olympic and world record. In the last event, the high jump, she cleared the bar in a record-breaking performance, but was disqualified from the gold because of her style (the head over heels technique preferred today).

She went on to learn golf, developing into a world-class amateur golfer. In that game of nerves, she once won 17 tournaments in row! In 1953 she developed cancer, had a reprieve and then went back to golfing. She won the Ben Hogan trophy for the greatest comeback in 1955. Dying of recurrent cancer at the age of 42, her life is an enduring example of someone who seemed to want to develop every talent that she had and use them for as long as she could.

"After a long time the master of those servants returned and settled accounts with them. The man who had received the five talents brought the other five. 'Master,' he said, 'you entrusted me with five talents. See, I have gained five more.'

"His master replied, 'Well done, good and faithful servant! You have been faithful with a few things; I will put you in charge of many things. Come and share your master's happiness!'"

MATTHEW 25:19-23

Jesus told this famous parable using financial terms to teach us that God is most concerned that we fully use all the gifts that he has given to us. In the athletic arena Babe Didriksen was a five-talent woman, and from all indications she used them all and got more. In the spiritual realm few of us may be five-talent people, but whether we are or not, we are called to develop *everything we have* for God. It is selfish and wrong to hoard our talents and not use them to build up God's church. It is wrong to have five and use only two. It is wrong to have two and use only one. It is wrong to have one and to hide it in the ground.

> *Each one should use whatever gift he has received to serve others, faithfully administering God's grace in its various forms (1 Peter 4:10).*

God does give each one of us gifts and talents—qualities we have in greater measure than others. For some, the gift is to encourage, for others to serve, and still others to lead. Some God has blessed with financial gifts so that we can contribute to the needs of others. Some, like Babe, have been blessed with athletic talent, others with administrative acumen, and still others with the ability to act. Some have a deep sense of compassion and the capacity to listen intently. Others have an endearing quality that allows them to quickly become everyone's "best friend." Still others have the proficiency to teach and instruct, aiding others to grow in their understanding of God's word. Regardless of what gifts God has given you, what you have is needed. It is important to realize how you can use your gifts to serve others.

Babe was not content with a few successes. She tried and excelled in basketball, running, the javelin, hurdles, the high jump, and golf. In the same way, we are not limited to a single gift or talent or, for that matter, even the gifts we have when we enter the kingdom. God is great at "multiplying our talents." He delights in turning our weaknesses into strengths. As we give ourselves wholeheartedly to his mission, he can add to the talents we already have. A sister can enter the kingdom a wallflower and yet, through God's power, become a person who inspires others. A brother can be baptized as an undisciplined derelict and be transformed into an example of reliability. The challenge is not to get comfortable where we are, but to deny ourselves and grow. Find someone whose talents you desire, learn from them and grow (Luke 6:40).

INTO YOUR LIFE

1. Do you know what your talents are? (If you are unsure, ask several people who know you well.)

2. In what ways can you use the gifts God has given you? Brainstorm! Let your mind go wild with ideas of how to serve God's kingdom. Formulate an action plan and start today.

3. Have you hoarded some of your talents and gifts? Have you been unwilling to deny yourself and give in the ways in which God has enabled you? If so, study out the parable of the talents in Matthew 25:14-30.

4. In what areas have you seen yourself grow since becoming a disciple? Have these become your gifts? In what areas do you want to grow?

Week Two

PEOPLE

THE POWER OF TEAM

Team U.S.A.
· HOCKEY ·
1980 Olympic Games

When Coach Herb Brooks envisioned the 1980 U.S. Olympic hockey team, he did not see the world's best individual hockey players. He saw *team*. He had only seven months to forge that team.

Many Olympic hockey teams, most notably the 1980 Soviet team, had been playing together for years. Described by sports writers as a "machine," the Soviet team had dominated Olympic hockey for 16 years, even defeating the National Hockey League All-Stars in a 1979 exhibition.

In 1979 Coach Brooks set out to select the young men who would make up the 1980 U.S. Olympic team from sixty-eight of the best amateur players in the country. Convening the tryouts, the coach began with an unorthodox test. It was not physical; it was mental—a written examination of more than 300 questions. The coach was not looking for the best individual players. He was looking for players who were willing to learn, to change, to be molded into a team.

Having winnowed the twenty-six team members, the coach taught them a new style of play designed to take advantage of the Olympic rink. Brooks called the new style "sophisticated pond hockey."

Unequal to the talent of the Soviets, the American team went after conditioning. Coach Brooks adapted stamina-building techniques from swimming and track, sports in which the Americans were stiff competition for the Soviets. Unafraid to be feared, the coach saw his unchallenged leadership and the toughness of their training as the prime way to unify the team.

Attitude was crucial. Brooks had chosen players so young and inexperienced that they were not awed by the other teams. They did not care that the world thought their cause hopeless, even after the Soviet team trounced them in exhibition play. They were excited to have a chance to do their best.

In Lake Placid, the Americans were seeded seventh of twelve teams. Coming from behind *in every game*, the team did something no one had believed they could do—they earned a place in the medal round. Then, playing on George Washington's birthday, they beat the Soviet team, astonishing themselves and the world. Two days later, they bested the Finns for the gold.

Not the best individual players in the world, not even the best individual players in the United States, they won *as a team* in a championship many will never forget.

...so in Christ we who are many form one body, and each member belongs to all the others.

ROMANS 12:5

From him the whole body, joined and held together by every supporting ligament, grows and builds itself up in love, as each part does its work.

EPHESIANS 4:16

Who would you pick for your team if you decided to change the world? When Jesus started his ministry, he did not start with the most awe-inspiring, spiritual, knowledgeable men in the world, but rather he was looking for people who were willing to learn, to change, to be molded. He knew success would not come from a few star performers but from finding those who would learn how to work in unity as a team.

Jesus' method of choice was unorthodox. All night he labored in prayer with his Father to select twelve men out of the crowds that were following him (Mark 3:13). The twelve he chose were an unlikely lot: several fishermen, a tax collector, a zealot—mostly unschooled and ordinary men. The more established Jewish "machine" paid no attention for a while. The Romans took no notice at all.

But spiritual training was underway. Jesus put a priority on relationship building. He taught his team to resolve their conflicts quickly and thoroughly (Matthew 5:23-26; Matthew 18:15-17). He taught them to be quick to forgive, even as God forgives (Matthew 18:21-35). He taught them about the special power that comes from praying together (Matthew 18:19-20). He taught that the one great distinguishing mark of those who followed him would be their amazing and sacrificial love for one another (John 13:34-35). He used the fishing analogy to teach them about their evangelistic mission—but remember that he chose this metaphor for men who knew only of fishing *in groups with nets*, because there were no solo fishermen with rods and reels in those days! When he said they would be "fishers of men," they would have understood the importance of working *together* in unity (Matthew 4:19-22; Luke 5:4-6).

At the end he gave them their final challenge: "...go into all the world and make disciples of all nations..." (Matthew 28:19). And make disciples they did. With uncompromising loyalty to Jesus and one another, they defeated stronghold after stronghold in the name of Christ, changing forever the face of the world and bringing the opportunity for salvation to all men.

The success of the American hockey team is a tribute to a determined coach and the spirit of teamwork he forged. It was the same with Jesus on a far grander scale. And that same Jesus is still teaching us today the power of unity and teamwork.

INTO YOUR LIFE

1. What questions might be on Jesus' test to determine if we are good candidates for team play? How would you do with those?

2. Consider Galatians 5:19-21. Notice that almost half of the listed sins interfere directly with successful teamwork. Are there any sins listed here that you have in your life? If so, what must you do?

3. Are there any members of the spiritual team you aren't united with? What can you do? How much are you willing to do to change that?

4. What things do you know you cannot accomplish for God without the help of others?

From Dull to Daring

Emil Zátopek
· DISTANCE RUNNER ·
Czechoslovakia

Emil Zátopek lived in the town of Zlin in Moravia and worked in the chemistry lab of a shoe company. Every spring the company sponsored races and all able-bodied residents were exhorted to run. The story is told that in 1941 Zátopek was not keen on the whole idea and hid himself in the town library. But someone found him and cajoled him until he took his place at the starting line. The improbable was about to happen.

Zátopek finished second in the town race and soon was training for more serious competition. His times rapidly improved, and many of his countrymen stood in awe of his ability. In 1948 he went to the London Olympic Games and brought home the gold medal for the 10,000-meter run and the silver for the 5,000. After watching Zátopek, one American sportswriter wrote that he was "gasping, clawing at his abdomen, bobbing, weaving, staggering, gyrating, flinging supplicating glances towards the heavens." There was apparently nothing boring about Emil Zátopek! He had become a passionate runner who knew how to win.

Four years later in Helsinki, he would do greater things. This time he won the gold in both the 10,000 and 5,000 becoming only the second man in history to do so. The second victory came on the same day that his wife, Dana, won the gold in the javelin. Dana thought the Zátopeks with their three golds were finished with the competition, but as they celebrated that night, Emil, as an afterthought, decided to run the marathon and try to do what no man had ever done: win the gold in the three longest races in the Games.

Not being familiar with this race, he asked Jim Peters of Great Britain if he could run beside him. At one point in the race Zátopek said to Peters, "Isn't this pace too fast?" Peters answered that it was too slow. Zátopek believed him and ran away from Peters and everyone else and on to the gold medal.

Whoever found Emil Zátopek hiding in the library of an obscure town, gave the Olympic Games one of its greatest champions—a hungry runner with passion and zeal.

*The angel of the L*ord *came and sat down under the oak in Ophrah that belonged to Joash the Abiezrite, where his son Gideon was threshing wheat in a winepress to keep it from the Midianites. When the angel of the L*ord *appeared to Gideon, he said, "The L*ord *is with you, mighty warrior."*

JUDGES 6:11-12

Somewhere out there in the libraries and winepresses (and living rooms) of the world, there are people who look ordinary, apathetic and boring. They have no dreams, no drive and no direction. But those dreary looking people are full of potential. Someone who probably didn't know what he was doing found Emil Zátopek. A God who knew exactly what he was doing found Gideon and turned the "least of the least" into a spiritual legend and a member of the faith hall of fame (Hebrews 11:32).

The way we look at ourselves can be so wrong. The way we look at others can be so wrong. We can see only the negatives, weaknesses and humanness, and we can forget what a man or a woman can become if they have a fire lit inside. Something lit Emil Zátopek's fire. God lit Gideon's fire. And God is eager to start some more. He is eager to take more dull people and turn them into passionate runners for him who "gasp, claw, gyrate, and fling supplicating glances—*and loud prayers*—towards heaven." He wants to find some more people in winepresses and libraries and fill them with a love for the battle and hunger to be a part of a spiritual army that attacks the gates of Hades.

The gospel is still the power of God. The message of the cross can take the dullest, the most indifferent and fill them with spiritual fervor so they will never be lacking in zeal (Romans 12:11). Likewise, it can take the crude and make them sensitive, the selfish and make them caring, the proud and make them humble, the most humanistic and make them spiritual. Look around you. Who is hiding in a library, a winepress, a kitchen, a living room, an office cubicle, a corporate office? Do you see what they can become? Do you realize you are God's match sent to start the fire?

Maybe you need to first let God find you. Maybe you need to see yourself as the person God meant you to be. Maybe you need to decide that there is one thing you will never be—a dull disciple. Maybe you need some prayer time of your own in which you "gasp and claw and fling some loud cries to heaven." Paul's words to Timothy may just be the ones you need: "For this reason I remind you to fan into flame the gift of God, which is in you through the laying on of my hands" (2 Timothy 1:6). We can't light any fires until we are on fire ourselves.

Emil's story is one of a changed life. In the world, stories like his are rare, and in the end his crown will not last. The gospel of God produces many stories of changed lives, and the crowns never fade or perish.

INTO YOUR LIFE

1. Is there any way in which you have been hiding in the "library" or the "winepress," not wanting to get into the race? If so, has anybody tried to coax you into action? How did you make them feel?

2. Do you believe people can change? How about that they can change from "dull" to "daring"? Do you believe you can change? What do you believe it takes?

3. If you were to become in your spiritual life what Zátopek was in his running, what would your prayer life look like? How does that compare with what it is today?

4. Who is someone you know outside the kingdom who is hiding from God's plan for their lives? How can you draw them out? What kinds of hospitality could warm their heart to the gospel?

SET AN EXAMPLE

Olga Korbut
· GYMNASTICS ·
Soviet Union (Byelorussia)

Imagine a girl who is 4'11" tall and weighs 85 pounds. Think of someone you know who is that size. Now envision that person being named the world's greatest female athlete by the Associated Press. That is exactly what happened to Olga Korbut in 1972, and single-handedly, she changed the attitude of an entire generation toward her sport.

Olga was from the city of Grodno in Byelorussia about 300 miles west of Moscow. She was only nine when she followed in the footsteps of a sister and joined a gymnastics club. Eight years later she would capture the love and attention of the world as she competed for the gold in the 1972 Olympics held in Munich, Germany.

Olga's training under a demanding perfectionist, Renald Kynsh, often resulted in tears and outbursts on her part. While she showed great promise, her first two years of serious competition brought no real victories. However, in 1972 things changed dramatically, and she won her way onto the Soviet team.

In Munich, Olga's opening performance in the all-around competition was disastrous. During her uneven bars performance she made three major mistakes, including an actual slip off the bars. She was visibly upset and wept openly. Ironically, it was these mistakes that would first endear her to the public. With these tears and later her unmistakable smile, she shattered the many false Cold War stereotypes concerning what Soviets were like.

While she showed emotions, she did not give in to them. She got back up on the uneven bars and won the silver medal during the individual competition. Next, she took the gold medal on the balance beam. Although she had modified her floor exercise program just five days before, she won yet another gold medal in this event. She topped it off by adding a third gold medal in the all-around team competition.

In the mid-70s, the number of would-be gymnasts in America grew from 15,000 to more than 50,000. The rise and popularity of the sport can be primarily attributed to the inspiration and charm of a seventeen-year-old Russian girl named Olga Korbut. Before Olga, gymnastic clubs were desperate for members—after Olga, they had to turn people away.

Thousands of young women, like Olympian Mary Lou Retton, were inspired by Olga's example to dream of winning Olympic gold and were motivated to work to see those dreams come true.

Don't let anyone look down on you because you are young, but set an example for the believers in speech, in life, in love, in faith and in purity.
1 TIMOTHY 4:12

It is a simple fact: People are inspired and motivated by other people. One person's inspirational example can change

- the way an individual looks at things
- the way a family looks at things
- the way a group looks at things

- the way a whole church looks at things
- the way an entire movement looks at things.

Regardless of our height or our weight, regardless of our youth or our age, regardless of our health or our lack of it, regardless of our education or our lack of it, *we can be examples*. Our lives can inspire others. Take it personally: *You* can inspire others.

Don't say, "But, I'm too young." In the above passage written to Timothy, Paul was telling him not to say that. Paul would have been equally firm with those who said, "But I'm too old" or "I'm too sick" or "I'm too ordinary." Paul believed that we can all "set an example for the believers in speech, in life, in love, in faith and in purity."

To the older disciples he would essentially say "be an example, live the life, and then teach the younger ones to do it too" (see Titus 2:1-4). To the sick he would in essence say, "God's power is made perfect in weakness. Be an example of faith in the midst of trial. You may inspire more people as a sick person than as a well one if you handle it by trusting God." To the ordinary, Paul might say, "Remember the words I wrote to another church":

> *Brothers, think of what you were when you were called. Not many of you were wise by human standards; not many were influential; not many were of noble birth. But God chose the foolish things of the world to shame the wise; God chose the weak things of the world to shame the strong. He chose the lowly things of this world and the despised things—and the things that are not—to nullify the things that are (1 Corinthians 1:26-28).*

Paul reminds us that God glories in the ordinary. God loves to use shepherds, tentmakers, fishermen and homemakers.

You may never get on worldwide television. Your name may never become a household word. But your example can influence others. Your faith in the midst of trial will be remembered by someone. Your love will lodge in someone's heart for years, influencing the way they love others. Your determination to make a disciple may cause someone to be reached who will in turn reach hundreds or thousands with the gospel. You don't know how far your example will go. You don't know how many lives it will touch. Your task is to be radically faithful and to let God create the impact he wants to create.

INTO YOUR LIFE

1. When was the last time you allowed others to know the hurt or disappointment you were feeling? How does it affect your relationships when you are vulnerable about your hurts? How does it affect your relationships when you are guarded?

2. Fill in the blank with what you might be tempted to think: "I am too _____ for God to use me." Do you believe that you can inspire others with your life if you ignore and overcome such thoughts?

3. Who do you think of as great examples of overcoming difficulties or adversities and allowing God to use their lives to his glory? Let them know how much they inspire and encourage you.

ETERNAL FRIENDSHIP

Shuhei Nishada & Sueo Oe
· POLE VAULT ·
Japan

The year was 1936. The place was the new Olympic stadium in Berlin—the house that Hitler himself had built to
showcase his superior German athletes. Competition had
been going on all day, and now it was late and raining. The
pole vault was the one event not yet completed. The unde-
cided contest was primarily between American Earl Meadows and two Japanese men who were teammates—and also
close friends—Shuhei Nishada and Sueo Oe. There were not
many left in the stadium to cheer the men on as night fell.

Soon Earl Meadows cleared the height of 14' 3 1/4"—a new
Olympic record. Both of the Japanese men missed all three
attempts at the bar, and the gold medal went to the American.

Shuhei Nishada and Sueo Oe continued to battle it out
for the silver and bronze when the judges called the contest
because of darkness.

Without explanation, the following day Nishada was
awarded the silver medal and Oe the bronze. They were both
shocked by the decision of the judges, feeling as though they
had performed with equality. But as courteous competitors,

they submitted themselves to the final decision and proudly stood and collected their prizes.

After the two returned to Japan, Nishada wanted to split his silver medal with his close friend. Oe agreed, and they split their individual medals in two and gave half to one another. Each man ended up with something unique in Olympic history: *a medal that was half silver and half bronze.* Appropriately, they called their new medals "the medals of eternal friendship."

Nishada and Oe understood that life is not just about winning—it is about sharing. They were great athletes, among the best in the world, but they understood that being great friends is of even more value.

After David had finished talking with Saul, Jonathan became one in spirit with David, and he loved him as himself. From that day Saul kept David with him and did not let him return to his father's house. And Jonathan made a covenant with David because he loved him as himself. Jonathan took off the robe he was wearing and gave it to David, along with his tunic, and even his sword, his bow and his belt.

1 SAMUEL 18:1-4

The story of Nishada and Oe reminds us of David and Jonathan. The biblical figures, like the Japanese duo, were involved in major events being followed with great interest by others. However, in the midst of much activity, and even turmoil, they took time to love one another as brothers. They understood two things we need to understand today: (1) God wants us to have great friendships and (2) when you have a great friendship, "it doesn't get any better than this."

Circumstances could have easily set David and Jonathan up to be fierce competitors. Most men in Jonathan's position—heir apparent—would have been threatened by David, one of the most popular Israelite warrior heroes. In a time when life was cheap, most would have quickly complied with the command of a jealous father king to take David's life. But Jonathan had the heart God wants us all to have: "...he loved [David] as he loved himself" (1 Samuel 18:1).

A little competition may be a lot of fun. But we are not primarily on earth to compete with one another; we are here to *love* one another. We are not here to beat one another; we are here to befriend one another. Games can be enjoyed. We can learn great lessons from athletes, from those who strive to win. (That is what this book is all about!) But if our desire to win puts distance between us and those around us, we have exchanged the greater for the lesser. If our desire to excel causes us not to care about our brother or our sister, we are excelling in things that will not last.

For the disciple there is an even more important thought here: In order for us to run, finish and win the Christian race, we must build great relationships and run the race side by side. Hear the words of our Lord and our coach: "A new command I give you: Love one another. As I have loved you, so you must love one another. By this all men will know that you are my disciples, if you love one another" (John 13:34-35). Great friendships are not something for us to build in heaven after the race is over. Great friendships will be instrumental in getting us to the finish line, and all who watch us run will see that we have them.

Jesus believed in friends. He put three years into forging friendships that would change the world. "Greater love has no one than this," he said in John 15:13, "that he lay down his life for his friends." True friendship involves paying a price. Sometimes the highest price. After Jesus' death and resurrection, we can be sure his disciples understood the word "friend" like never before. They appreciated what it meant to be loved, to have someone care even more about them than he cared about himself.

Today we cannot afford to just be *in* the church. We must be *great friends* in the church. We cannot afford to just know the Bible; we must build the relationships it guides us to build. If the price for that is high, so be it, for "it doesn't get any better than this."

INTO YOUR LIFE

1. List the people you would call your best friends. What are you thankful for in these relationships?

2. It has been said, "If you want great friends, be one." How does that statement challenge you and give you direction?

3. List some people (not on the list above) that you want to befriend. What can you do for them that will impact their lives?

4. If your friendships aren't where they need to be, what can you begin to do to turn things around?

NOT WITHOUT COACHING

Herb Elliot
· TRACK ·
Australia

As a child, Herb Elliott loved to race, and he loved to win. From the time he was eight he only lost one race to a boy three years older than himself, and from that point on, he never lost again. Herb Elliot was the wonder boy of running.

Herb was well on his way to competing with the world's best when in 1955, at the age of 17, Herb had a bizarre accident. A piano accidentally toppled over and crushed his foot. The accident also crushed his young spirit. He lost the heart to run and quit the sport.

But then, in stepped his parents. Wanting him to regain his love of running and believing in the power of inspiration, they arranged to bring him to the 1956 Olympic Games held in Melbourne. Watching men like Ron Delany of Ireland and Vladimir Kuts of Russia compete with heart and soul sparked the fire that Herb had lost, and soon he was running again.

Probably his most important decision was to place himself under the guidance and direction of coach Percy Cerutty who would test and challenge him like never before. Coach

Cerutty set a goal for Herb to break the four-minute-mile mark, and he did so within two years. By 1958 he was pitted against Ron Delany, the very same gold-medal miler who had inspired Herb at the Melbourne Games. He beat Delany at a U.S. event and set a new world record for the mile. Later he beat Delany in Ireland and before the year was out set a new world mark in the 1,500 meters.

Within a year, however, Herb was losing the fire *again* and was easing back on the training essential for world-class athletes. He even started smoking. Despite all of his wins, it appeared that Herb did not really have what it took to be an Olympic champion. But Coach Cerutty stepped in again and challenged him. It was what he needed. Herb "repented" and resumed serious training.

When the 1,500-meter finals were held at the Rome Olympic Games in 1960, Herb Elliott ran so fast that some said he looked like a scared bunny. His time of 3:35.6 was a new world record. Yet for all his raw talent and abilities, it took the help of many others: his family, his coach and even his competitors to truly bring out the champion in Herb Elliot.

As iron sharpens iron,
    so one man sharpens another.

PROVERBS 27:17

Instead, speaking the truth in love, we will in all things grow up into him who is the Head, that is, Christ.

EPHESIANS 4:15

Let the word of Christ dwell in you richly as you teach and admonish one another with all wisdom, and as you sing psalms, hymns and spiritual songs with gratitude in your hearts to God.

COLOSSIANS 3:16

Watch the Olympic Games. Pay careful attention to the things said about the athletes. In case after case you will hear something about those who coach them. Almost never will you find great athletes who got that way without coaching. A person may have incredible talent and a strong competitive drive, but without a good coach, it will usually go to waste. Even the greatest of athletes with years of experience still rely on the wisdom, help and input of coaches.

To reach our maximum performance we simply must have other people in our lives who are telling us what they see, challenging our wrong attitudes and calling us higher. The Bible could not be any clearer about this. We need people to sharpen us, people to tell us the truth and people to counsel and instruct us.

All of this grows out of a simple idea that every great athlete understands: *We simply cannot see ourselves objectively.* We may think we know ourselves well, and certainly we do have some "inside" information, but our emotions, biases and blind spots get in the way. We cannot be all we can be for God unless we get some good coaches in our lives. If we are too proud to admit that we need such help, our pride will end up being our destruction.

And what makes a good—athletic or spiritual—coach? First of all he (or she) is knowledgeable. He knows what works and what doesn't. He has seen defeat and knows what causes it. He has seen victory and knows what brings it. Second, he is not sentimental. He is tough minded. He is not afraid of challenging you to do hard things. He wants you to succeed more than he wants you to feel comfortable. Third, he doesn't give up. Coach Cerutty saw his star drifting away, but he did not lose his vision for him. He kept holding it before him and calling him to it. A good coach will still be there, even when we are down.

But there is another side of the coin. Many of us need to *be* spiritual coaches, while still being coached ourselves. "By this time you ought to be teachers," admonished the writer of Hebrews (5:12). He was talking to people who had been around long enough and had enough experience that they should have been training and discipling others. Right now in many of our lives there are others who depend on us. They need our involvement. They need us to speak the truth to them. They need our encouragement. Being there for others helps them stay in the race and off the dropout list.

INTO YOUR LIFE

1. What experiences have helped you see your personal need for coaching?

2. What attitudes are in your life that are currently making you easy to coach?

3. What should you do if no one is taking that much interest in coaching or training you?

4. Who is relying on you for input, advice, counsel? Are they getting from you what they need?

THE IMPACT OF FAMILY

Jackie Joyner-Kersee
· HEPTATHALON, LONG JUMP ·
United States

East St. Louis, Illinois, has been called "a city of no hope." For many, it is the inner city of inner cities, the ghetto of ghettos. Characterized by darkness, drugs, despair and death, it spawns few celebrities. But in a city of no hope, one mother captured and held on to hope. She would not let it escape, and she passed it on to her daughter, Jackie Joyner. Firm in her faith, she was also firm in the discipline of her children. In a neighborhood in which little was expected, Ms. Joyner expected much. She was like a "velvet brick"—hard-lined, yet endearingly loving.

In such a home environment, Jackie and her brothers were secure and determined to succeed. In her inner-city high school, she excelled in volleyball and basketball. The effect of her home life was unmistakable. Her coach put it succinctly: "All the support Jackie needed at home was there."

After earning an athletic scholarship to UCLA, this multi-talented woman not only played basketball, but participated in track and field events as well. Her natural talent and determination, combined with the support of a new relationship with the assistant track coach, showed her to be a champion-in-the-making. Bob Kersee became the love of her life and the best trainer an Olympic hopeful could have.

While she was winning her first medal, a silver in the heptathlon in the 1984 summer games in Los Angeles, her brother was there, as well. He led the way with his gold-medal performance in the triple jump.

Jackie and Bob married in the summer of 1986. More than ever, the two were one: trainer and athlete, husband and wife. That summer she set the American record in the heptathlon. By the 1988 games held in Seoul, Jackie felt more ready then ever to compete for the gold. The heptathlon's seven events are grueling for the healthiest of athletes, but Jackie had an additional problem in that she suffered from exercise-induced asthma. With the encouragement that only a family can give, Jackie overcame all odds and performed brilliantly. Not only did she win the individual long jump event, but she took home a gold for the heptathlon. Her final point tally of 7,291 was an Olympic milestone record. Many thought the 7,000 mark would never be reached.

Amazingly, Jackie returned to the Olympics in 1992 to compete in the heptathlon as a 30-year-old. Many chalked her off as a has-been and gave her no chance of winning. But, they did not know Jackie-Joyner Kersee *or* the woman who gave her birth, both of whom paid no attention to the critics. From East St. Louis to Barcelona, they beat the odds every time. Once again she was a winner.

These commandments that I give you today are to be upon your hearts. Impress them on your children. Talk about them when you sit at home and when you walk along the road, when you lie down and when you get up.

Deuteronomy 6:6-7

Through God's wise design, he endowed parents with great power in the lives of their children. From the moment of birth, the parents' love, or lack of it, is communicated clearly to this new little person. God meant for home to be a place of safety, security and spirituality. He wanted it to be a place where children would begin to learn about his nature as a loving father.

Jackie Joyner-Kersee's mom "caught the drift." She knew the kind of impact she was able to have on her children. She believed in God and she believed in the children he gave her. In a soil of despair, she planted hope. No excuses. No giving up. And the hope grew, taking Jackie along with it. Because of her home, she could see beyond the ghetto. She could see beyond crumbling buildings, warring gangs, dirty streets. She saw more than trash caught in hot gusts of wind. She could see greatness in the distance.

Home will not be what God intended if parents do not first set their own priorities straight. They will never be able to point their children to true greatness, a relationship with Jesus Christ, unless they have found it themselves. They will never be able to plant the seeds of victory unless they have found victory themselves. In Deuteronomy 6, before the injunction to teach their children, parents are told,

> *Love the LORD your God with all your heart and with all your soul and with all your strength. These commandments that I give you today are to be upon your hearts (Deuteronomy 6:5-6).*

Certainly God knew that if they didn't have it, they couldn't give it.

Parents must see beyond challenging circumstances, busy schedules, financial difficulties. They must go after God with all their hearts. They must live their faith when they first get up in the morning. No excuses. No "Wait till I have my coffee." They must live it when their children disappoint them.

They must live it when they are annoyed with solicitors on the phone, when they are tired and ready to go to bed. And most of all, they must live it when they have "blown it." They must be humble and confess their wrong. Perfection will never win their kids, only humility. They cannot just be "religious." Children are astute; they will know the difference.

Planting seeds of hope and victory is the greatest of all legacies. Our children may never win gold medals, but they will gain something far more valuable and far more enduring.

INTO YOUR LIFE

1. Think of a parent who is a great example of imparting their faith to their children. What can you learn from him or her about helping others to grow in their faith?

2. For parents: In which situations are you most tempted to let down your guard and not be a great example for your children? How often do you confess when you blow it?

For others: Which children do you have an opportunity to influence? How aware are you of your responsibility to them?

3. What have you had to overcome in your background that could have kept you from receiving the victory that Jesus offers? How has he helped you overcome?

4. What character trait keeps you from having a greater impact on your family? Who is helping you with this? What coaching are you getting?

THE POWER OF TWO

Dick and Rick Hoyt
• MARATHON, TRIATHALON •
United States

You will not find Dick or Rick Hoyt's names in any of the official record books. Neither of them ever made an Olympic team, but they are full of the Olympic spirit and you can see in both of them the heart of a champion. Father and son, Dick and Rick Hoyt are a familiar sight to the crowds that line the streets each April to watch the famed Boston Marathon. Many come just to see them, to catch a glimpse of this extraordinary team, these unlikely heroes. Although Rick is severely paralyzed by Cerebral Palsy, he sits tall in his specially designed wheelchair as his father pushes him through the grueling 26-mile course.

In his 34 years, Rick has never walked, talked or fed himself, but with the help of his parents, his physical needs have always been met. On the other hand, Dick never saw himself as one who had the drive and determination necessary for athletic achievement. But his son's spirit has more than made up Dick's deficiencies of character. Together the Hoyt duo form one athlete's body and one athlete's heart—apart from each other they would never compete. Together they amaze and inspire all who see them.

Year after year, they have entered and finished marathons all over the United States. They even added triathlons to their repertoire with Dick towing Rick on a raft, no easy feat for a man who finally learned to swim in his fifties! But as Dick Hoyt says, "When we're out there [competing], there's nothing I feel I can't do with Rick." Rick recently graduated from Boston University (proving he is not just another jock!), and he and his dad just completed their latest remarkable exploit—a bicycle ride across America.

Two are better than one,
because they have a good return for their work:
If one falls down,
his friend can help him up.
But pity the man who falls
and has no one to help him up!

ECCLESIASTES 4:9-10

The profile of two: When I am weak, you are strong; when you are weak, I am strong. A profound power. A simple truth. A shared strength. The wise author of Ecclesiastes describes it clearly.

Jesus, the author and source of every true principle, certainly knew the power of two. Luke tells us "After this the Lord appointed seventy-two others and sent them two by two ahead of him to every town and place where he was about to go" (Luke 10:1). He wanted his messengers to go in pairs to spread the news of his coming kingdom. When one would be discouraged, the other would be called upon to be full of zeal. When one would be full of doubt, the other would feel the need to be full of decisive faith. If one fell down, his friend would be there to pick him up.

Dick and Rick Hoyt have surely needed to rely on each other in a unique way. In fact, they probably define the power of two in as great a way as any pair could. Their unity of determination brings tears to the eyes of the spectators. Many wave them on to victory, finding themselves too overcome with emotion to even cheer. In a self-centered world where everyone seems to look out for number one, it is a moving sight to see two work together as one.

When the seventy-two in Luke 10 returned two by two just as they had been sent out, Jesus felt emotion. The Scriptures say he was actually "full of joy through the Holy Spirit" (v. 21) as he received and encouraged these little teams. Each disciple had gone out with another, and in unity they had worked together to smash the forces of darkness (v. 17). He knew all along that two disciples united under his name produces one Satan falling like lightning from heaven (v. 18), but he was clearly moved to hear the reports of how it happened. Even God rejoices to see spiritual truth put into practice.

But being part of a twosome has another benefit that is not always so welcome. It will at times reveal our laziness or our commitment, our reluctance or our eagerness, our "ho-humness" or our zeal. We cannot hide behind the faceless crowd. Whether in marriage, in any coleading situation, or simply in one-on-one friendships, the best is demanded, and our hearts will be tested.

Being teamed up with another person can cause us fear, especially if we are hiding something that we do not want others to know or if we are content to be superficial and unspiritual. We may want to "go it alone" if we are not eager or willing to "think of others more highly" than we think of ourselves. When such tendencies surface, we must not give in to the flesh. We need times with others to push such things to the surface so they can be dealt with forcefully.

We need partners to strengthen us when our spiritual legs don't seem to work or when our unspiritual minds and hearts are working *too* much. The God who created the universe as a "We" longs for us to know the power of two. He is eager for us to drop our independence and to allow ourselves to unite with others so the strength of his whole body, the church, will be doubled and tripled and made ready for the task he has for it: to make disciples of all nations.

INTO YOUR LIFE

1. In which relationships are you paired with someone? How do you respond to that pairing? What have you learned about yourself because of it?

2. How does it affect your spiritual life when you have an attitude that says, "I can do it all by myself"?

3. How are you affected by the story of the Hoyts? Are there any spiritual situations where you need to follow their example? Be specific. Could you be content being either the father or the son?

4. What attitudes need to be in your life so that being paired up with you would mean joy and encouragement to someone else? Are these attitudes in your heart or is repentance needed?

Week Three

PASSION

ALL THINGS ARE POSSIBLE

Bob Beamon
·LONG JUMP·
United States

In the qualifying round of the long-jump competition held in Mexico City in 1968, favorite Bob Beamon looked as if he might not even make it into the finals, much less win a medal. Beamon had fouled on his first two of three attempts. One more foul and he would be eliminated from the competition.

His teammate and good friend, Ralph Boston, saw his need for help and encouragement, and had a pep talk with Beamon before his final jump. Boston was an incredible jumper who was the current holder of the world record. He was also the first jumper to break the mark that Jessie Owens had set in the 1938 Berlin games. Reminiscent of the advice given by Luz Long to Jessie Owens at that Olympiad, Boston told Beamon to jump at least one foot back of the foul line so there would be no danger of a foul. The advice paid off and Beamon moved into the finals. Long-jump records are sometimes broken by inches and more often by parts of an inch. At that time Boston's world long-jump record stood at 27' 4 3/4". And although jumpers were gaining ground on the 28' mark, this seemed like a lofty goal to most—a "maybe" or "some-day" goal.

On his first jump, Beamon raced down the runway and leaped into the pit. He knew immediately it was a great jump. He was sure he had broken Boston's record, but he had no idea how incredible the jump really was. The electronic measuring device that was in place would not measure that far—a measuring tape would need to be used. But once the markings were taken, the new world record would be 29' 2½"—nearly 2 feet over Boston's record! The long jump record from Owens to Boston, a period of over thirty-three years, had advanced by 8½ inches. With his jump, Beamon had advanced the record by 21¾ inches. When the announcement was made, many were sure there was some mistake. The other competitors were in shock.

The impossible had happened. Prior to the 1968 Olympics you would have found few who believed a man could jump 28 feet. Bob Beamon had jumped over 29 feet and set a record no one thought would ever be broken.

Jesus looked at them and said, "With man this is impossible, but with God all things are possible."
MATTHEW 19:26

Listen to these words spoken recently by a brother in Christ: "I feel paralyzed by fears. I feel crippled by my own insecurities. I see my sin and struggle even to believe that God will continue loving me—much less continue using me or helping me change. My sin is that bad. How can I ever hope to stand up under it? Failure after failure after failure... What hope could there possibly be for someone such as me?"

Have you ever been there? Faced with life's failures, it is often hard to stay in the fight. Just having two or three weeks of victory in any area may seem impossible to some people.

They decided to follow Jesus Christ, but now they feel like anything but spiritual champions.

But God loves the impossible. God has a plan for us—a plan to help us overcome our sins and lead powerful lives. It may seem impossible. The deck may seem stacked against us. But we make a terrible mistake when we limit the one who can do more than we could ever ask or imagine by our failure to believe.

"If you believe, you will receive whatever you ask for in prayer" (Matthew 21:22). Do you doubt? Does overcoming seem "impossible" to you? Read the Scriptures. *Really* get into them. One thing that seems to pop up over and over again is that God really enjoys exceeding the wildest expectations of his people. The waters parted, the sun stopped in its course, the lame walked, the blind received sight, the dead rose, and the sinners were given new lives (that's us).

In light of God's power, everything is possible. You can do so much more than just overcome your struggles with sin (although this is a miracle of God in itself). You can help change the world. You can be a vital part of something that powerfully impacts the lives of thousands throughout generations. More can happen "than all we ask or imagine" (Ephesians 3:20-21).

Too often we set out just trying not to "foul out" when God's plan is to set new records with our lives. Allow your life to be a testimony to God's power by allowing him to transform you, to take hold of you. Is God calling you to do something scary right now? Something you don't think you can do? Something you have tried to do and have failed to do? Pray for faith. Listen to faithful friends. Then leap with faith. There is no way to measure the impact you will have.

> *"'If you can'?" said Jesus. "Everything is possible for him who believes."*
>
> *Immediately the boy's father exclaimed, "I do believe; help me overcome my unbelief!" (Mark 9:23-24).*

INTO YOUR LIFE

1. In what ways has God overcome "impossible" circumstances in twentieth century? What stories have you heard about God doing the impossible? How do these increase your faith in facing current challenges?

2. Take a very careful look at your own life. What are some "impossible" things that have already happened? (If you cannot think of anything, read Matthew 19:25-26 again very carefully, and think about what has happened to you.)

3. Do failures in your life seem to set up impossible situations? Is there anything you want to see happen in your life as a disciple but doubt that it can happen because of past failures? What does God have to say about such thinking?

4. Are you just trying to make the jump, or are you going for the gold? What is "more than you can imagine" in your life? Do you believe that God can accomplish this? How do you pray to overcome unbelief?

5. No one thought Bob Beamon could jump over 29 feet. Beamon himself never dreamed he could do that. If God chooses to bring them about, what are some "impossible" things that could still happen in your life?

Rafer Johnson
· DECATHLON ·
United States

When Robert F. Kennedy was fatally shot while campaigning for President in California, his friend, Rafer Johnson, was at his side. This painful loss was not the first dark hour in his life. He had suffered a history of setbacks that would have discouraged and frustrated most athletes to the point of giving up—but for Johnson, quitting was not an option.

As a young boy, he almost lost part of his foot in a conveyor-belt accident. Doctors were able to save his toes, and he recovered enough to become a four-sport athlete in high school. Johnson excelled in the classroom as well as on the field and earned a scholarship to UCLA. It was at UCLA that Johnson first began to train and compete in the ten-event decathlon, the most demanding of all the Olympic events. He was a fast learner, and in only his fourth decathlon competition, he broke the world record. Johnson earned a spot on the 1956 Olympic team and was a serious contender for a gold medal in the decathlon, and also the long jump, that year.

Then injury hit—the first of many. During the decathlon, he injured his knee and was not able to compete in the long jump. He continued in the decathlon, but during the discus throw he tore one of his abdominal muscles. Johnson would not see the gold. Returning to UCLA, he began to train under coach Ducky Drake to prepare for the 1960 Olympiad in Rome, setting another world record in the process. World-class decathlete C.K. Yang from Taiwan became both his teammate and roommate as they trained together to compete for the gold. But then came 1959 and a near fatal car crash and serious injuries. Johnson recovered but had to wait until five months before the Games to resume serious training.

In the Olympic trials, Johnson regained his form and set a new world record. Later in Rome in the Olympic finals, he found himself part of a two-man contest with his friend and teammate, C. K. Yang, now representing his native Taiwan. The events were dramatic with the lead swinging back and forth several times. At the start of the final event, the 1500-meter run, Johnson had the lead by 67 points. To win the gold, Yang would have to win by at least eight seconds. Yang's best time was better than Johnson's best by eighteen seconds. But Johnson ran an incredible race, clinging to Yang the whole way and finishing just 1.2 seconds behind. Johnson had come back again and beat the odds to be called the "world's greatest athlete."

Not only so, but we also rejoice in our sufferings, because we know that suffering produces perseverance; perseverance, character; and character, hope. And hope does not disappoint us, because God has poured out his love into our hearts by the Holy Spirit, whom he has given us.

ROMANS 5:3-5

Consider it pure joy, my brothers, whenever you face trials of many kinds, because you know that the testing of your faith develops perseverance.

JAMES 1:2-3

There is one word that best describes athletic injuries: *frustrating*. An athlete trains and prepares. He or she spends hours on the track, in the pool, on the court, in the gym, and then a muscle pulls, a tendon pops, torn cartilage has to be removed. The one who has prepared and trained, must now sit and watch. Or at least they must rehabilitate and go back to square one and start again. If they are not knocked out of the competition altogether, they have still lost valuable time. Injuries are a painful reminder (in more ways than one) that we are not totally in control of our own fate.

The bigger and more important race that all disciples run is seldom a string of victories with no setbacks. Along the way there are "injuries," trials, disappointments, heartaches. Someone we love and trust will let us down. Someone we had vision for will turn away and go back to the world. Some leader will misunderstand us and misjudge us. Someone in the world will malign our motives and accuse us of something terrible. Such things can hurt—deeply.

We may find our spiritual motivation low, our spiritual dreams deflated, our spiritual fervor drained out. It may take spiritual physicians and experts in spiritual rehabilitation to get us back on our feet, to get us running again. But it is times like these that show us where our hearts really are. If they knock us out of the race, our convictions were not as deep as we thought. If, on the other hand, we climb out of the "car wreck" and get back in the gym with Jesus Christ, we will become stronger than ever. If we start working again to reach our goals, we will develop *perseverance*, we will become people of *character*, and we will end up giving *hope* to a lot of people around us (Romans 5:3-5).

We have all been hurt, and we will all be hurt again. You see the difference in people's hearts in how they respond to the injuries. Some become fearful, faithless, distrustful, bitter and whiny. Others turn to God and say, "This hurts, Father, but teach me through this. Make me stronger through this. Keep me running for you through this."

Faith that cannot endure testing is worthless. It is shown not to be faith at all. Real faith gets bruised and battered and bloody, but it gets back up and stays in the fight. And ultimately, it becomes that which overcomes the world (1 John 5:3-4).

INTO YOUR LIFE

1. List some "injuries" you have experienced since becoming a disciple.

2. Describe your attitude toward these injuries.

3. What have you learned about how to handle such things? List three things you would want to teach a young Christian about growing through setbacks or trials.

4. How did Jesus handle the injuries in his life? In what ways do you want to follow in his steps?

HOLDING TO THE DREAM

Agnes Keleti
· GYMNASTICS ·
Hungary

At the age of 35, women are just hitting their peak in the business world, but not so in the Olympic world, especially in gymnastics. A coach maybe, but not a gymnast. But in 1956 in Melbourne, Australia, a 35-year-old Hungarian named Agnes Keleti was a true contender for gold. She truly believed she could win top honors; although many others felt she was way past her prime—not of the same caliber as the young breed. As a teenager in the late thirties, Agnes had dreamed of being part of the Hungarian Olympic gymnastic team, and in fact, she was their best hope when all talk of the Olympics came to an abrupt end. Hitler had started his European campaign and invaded Keleti's country in 1941. Being Jews in Nazi-occupied Hungary, her family tried to flee. All escaped through the underground except her father. He died in Auschwitz, a tortured Jew in the hands of an enemy.

Nonetheless, Keleti believed in her dream. With the war over, she once again set out for the Olympics. Although she made the team in 1948 as a 27-year-old, an injury kept her out of the competition. Four years later, at 31, she not only made the team again, she won a gold medal in the floor exercise.

In 1956 Hungary was again occupied—this time by the Soviet Communist machine. The idea of living under a restrictive political regime motivated her more than anything to try for the team once again. In Melbourne, Keleti did the unheard of, the impossible. *At age 35 she won four gold medals*—in balance beam, uneven bars, portable apparatus (no longer an event) and floor exercise. After the games she stayed in Australia and later married and moved to Israel. At age 42 she again went against the odds: She became a mother for the first time.

"Now then, just as the Lord promised, he has kept me alive for forty-five years since the time he said this to Moses, while Israel moved about in the desert. So here I am today, eighty-five years old! I am still as strong today as the day Moses sent me out; I'm just as vigorous to go out to battle now as I was then."
JOSHUA 14:10-11

Agnes Keleti's story of victory is reminiscent of the life of the Israelite, Caleb. Until the age of 38, he had lived as a slave in Egypt. Undoubtedly, he had every reason a man could have to feel worthless, defeated and hopeless. Yet he didn't. In Exodus and Numbers we can see the bitterness, resentment and distrust that took hold of his peers. Yet when 40-year-old Caleb was chosen with eleven others to survey the "promised land" for Israel, he said, "We should by all means go up and take possession of it, for we shall surely overcome it" (Numbers 13:30, NASB). Caleb returned with a gleam in his eye and a dream in his heart.

How frustrated he must have felt when the dream was smashed before his eyes because the Israelites revolted in cowardice. What pain Caleb must have felt to hear the sentence of God against his people because of their lack of faith (Numbers 14:20-35) and then to see his brothers die in the desert over the next 40 years!

Caleb was a man of a different spirit (Numbers 14:24). He had a spirit that trusted God and refused to let his dream die in spite of any barrier. He knew that with God, he and the Israelites could do anything that God asked them to do.

Forty-five years later, Caleb tells his story (Joshua 14:6-12). He was 80 years old before he saw the beginnings of his dream fulfilled. Then it took another five years of battling to fully realize the promise of God in receiving the land. For all that he had been through, he was able to say at 85 years of age, "I am still as strong today as I was in the day Moses sent me. As my strength was then, so my strength is now" (Joshua 14:11, NASB). Then Caleb went all out and asked for Hebron, the home of the giant Anakim, for his tribe's inheritance, saying, "Perhaps the Lord will be with me, and I shall drive them out as the Lord has spoken." And drive then out he did! (Joshua 15:13-19, NASB). Caleb was able to do what many today would think impossible: At age 85, rather than just being content to be in the "Olympics," he pulled out all the stops and took golds in warfare, leadership, optimism, vision, perseverance and obedience to God Almighty.

The dream of God is to save the entire world. It's a huge task, and there are many frustrations—especially those faithless persons surrounding us at work, our neighborhoods and even in the church. The Bible teaches that not one of the men living at the time of the initial spying of the land, except Joshua and Caleb, ever entered the land. This means that all the men who conquered the land were at least 40 years younger than Caleb! His dream and spirit made Caleb one of the most effective leaders of Israel, even among the younger, more energetic warriors! Agnes Keleti and the biblical Caleb show us that those who are determined can go beyond what is normal and see their dreams come true.

INTO YOUR LIFE

1. Recall the hopes and dreams you had when you were first baptized. Which ones have you realized? Which have you given up on? Which are you still holding on to?

2. What dreams do you need to get back?

3. What type of a "different spirit" do you think you need to have? Are you satisfied with being "normal"? How could you "go beyond what is normal"?

4. When the enemy says, "How dare you try that?" what is your response?

5. What excuses will you have to give up in order to do something amazing for God?

Straining Toward What Is Ahead

Ademar Ferreira da Silvia
· TRIPLE JUMP ·
Brazil

To set an Olympic or world record takes incredible drive. An athlete must strive not only to do his best, but he must also have the vision and confidence to believe that his best can be the best that has ever been done.

Brazilian triple jumper, Ademar Ferreira da Silvia was a man who possessed both of these qualities. In the summer games of 1952 in Helsinki, Ademar was a serious contender for a medal. The athletes of Brazil had never won a medal in Olympic history. The finals consisted of six jumps, and Ferreira da Silvia had a fierce determination to take home the gold, not only for himself, but for all of Brazil. In his first jump, Ferreira da Silvia set a new world record, which would prove enough for the gold medal. But Ferreira da Silvia was not satisfied. He knew that he could do more and take it even farther. He continued to jump, and when he finished his sixth and final jump, he had broken and set the world record *four times* in one competition!

He was able to return to the Games once again in 1956 and repeat his performance, winning another gold medal.

He made a final appearance in the Games in 1960 at the age of thirty-three. In his great career following the 1952 games, he won an incredible total of *sixty consecutive triple-jump competitions!* Ferreira da Silvia will continue to stand out in Olympic history as a man who wanted to be the best he could possibly be.

> *Not that I have already obtained all this, or have already been made perfect, but I press on to take hold of that for which Christ Jesus took hold of me. Brothers, I do not consider myself yet to have taken hold of it. But one thing I do: Forgetting what is behind and straining toward what is ahead, I press on toward the goal to win the prize for which God has called me heavenward in Christ Jesus.*
>
> PHILIPPIANS 3:12-14

At the time of this writing, Paul may very well have done more than any disciple of Jesus—living or dead—to advance the cause of the gospel throughout the world. He set some world records. He won some spiritual gold medals. The churches he planted, the converts he won, not to mention the abuse he took for the cross (see 2 Corinthians 11:24-28), cannot be rivaled. But, remarkably, he did not act as if he had arrived. He plainly said he had not.

He purposely "forgot" all his accomplishments, and he focused only on what he still could do and what he still could become. Like Ferreira da Silvia, he strained forward toward what was ahead. We need to be men and women who are so possessed.

Some of us could put together a pretty impressive spiritual résumé: given up some ugly sins, studied the Bible with a number of people, helped people become disciples, discipled others toward maturity, raised up some people to leadership, done some very good things to help the poor. Maybe we have planted a church or several churches. Maybe we have seen our children become Christians.

But what do we do now? Remind others of all those things we have done? Rest up and let others now carry the load? Or confess, "We are unworthy servants. We have only done our duty" (Luke 17:10)? And then give God our best today as though it were the very first day of our life in Christ?

There is no doubt that Ferreira da Silvia showed us in the Olympic arena an attitude that we must have in the kingdom of God. We must be thankful for what God has done, but never satisfied to stop with how he has used us. We must always be making ourselves available to him in *new ways*, asking him to take us places we have never gone and to do with us things that are greater and things that make *more* impact.

In 2 Corinthians 7:1 Paul called on the Corinthians to be all they could be. "Since we have these promises, dear friends, let us purify ourselves from *everything* that contaminates body and spirit, *perfecting holiness* out of reverence for God" (emphasis added). The first edition of the NIV translated this last phrase "striving for perfection out of reverence for God." And that really describes the attitude a true disciple will have. He knows his imperfections. He rejoices that God uses him in spite of those, but he seeks to get rid of everything that contaminates his body or his spirit. Because of his reverence for God, he cries out to God, "Search me, O God, and know my heart; test me and know my anxious thoughts. See if there is any offensive way in me, and lead me in the way everlasting (Psalm 139:23-24).

The New Testament is full of challenges for us to go farther than we have gone: "Be perfect, therefore, as your heavenly Father is perfect" (Matthew 5:48). "Be imitators of God, therefore, as dearly loved children and live a life of love, just as Christ loved us and gave himself up for us as a fragrant offering and sacrifice to God" (Ephesians 5:1-2). "To this you were called, because Christ suffered for you, leaving you an example, that you should follow in his steps" (1 Peter 2:21).

Complacency has no place in the life of a disciple!

INTO YOUR LIFE

1. By the grace of God, what good things have you been able to do in your life? What is your attitude toward those things?

2. Is there more evidence for the attitude of Ferreira da Silvia in your life or more evidence for complacency?

3. If during this next month you were to "strive for perfection out of reverence for God," what changes would be seen in your life?

4. Why is it so important to keep in mind "these promises" of God (2 Corinthians 7:1) as we seek to take it higher?

PRESSING THROUGH THE PAIN

Kip Keino
· DISTANCE RUNNER ·
Kenya

"I run with my heart, not with my legs." These are the words both spoken and lived by Olympic champion Kip Keino. His early years were filled with pain and heartache. He was the last child born to a mother who had previously lost every one of four children during childbirth. This was not uncommon in his small mountain village of Kapchemoylmo, Kenya. But even more tragic than those deaths was the loss of his mother when he was only four years old.

Kip began to race when he started school at the age of twelve. Although he started his education late, by eighteen he was able to join the Kenyan police force. He soon began to race for the police team and then in more competitive international races. By 1964, he had qualified for the Olympics as a long distance runner. Racing in the 5,000-meter that year, he came up just short of a medal.

By the 1968 Olympics, Kip had become a faster runner, qualifying for the finals of both the 5,000- and 10,000-meter races. In the 10,000-meter final, he was running a great race when he suddenly doubled over and sprawled out onto the grass in the throes of a gallbladder attack. The pain was agonizing. As medics ran toward him, he stumbled heroically to his feet. Although the pain had not subsided, he began to run again and finished the race.

Doctors cautioned him about any further competition under the circumstances, but Kip continued. He ran the 5,000 meters and won the silver medal. Then in the 1,500-meter race, he gave his all. He raced with pain, but he raced triumphantly. His margin of victory that day was so great that he set an Olympic record that would stand for the next twenty years. Kip Keino, the champion, meant it when he said, "I run with my heart, not with my legs."

For it is commendable if a man bears up under the pain of unjust suffering because he is conscious of God.

1 PETER 2:19

We run the Christian race with our hearts, not our legs. As disciples, we must hold on to our convictions and not be deterred by pain or suffering. As Kip Keino persevered through pain to set a record that would last for twenty years, our first-century brothers and sisters set a standard for us that endures even today. They faced incredible opposition because of their faith. Many were crucified or burned to death. Men watched their wives sentenced to death rather than deny their Lord. Mothers wept and witnessed their young children sewn into animal skins and attacked by wild beasts rather than disown their Lord.

We are called by their example to endure suffering however unjust it may be. The "persecution" many of us face pales in comparison to what the early disciples endured.

The person you had over for dinner last week refuses to return your calls. When you go by to see her, you discover that she heard negative things about the church and wants nothing to do with you. As you drive home, tasting the salt of your tears, you say to yourself, "We could have been such great friends."

A brother studies the Bible with his boss. The employer bucks at the thought of having to give up an immoral relationship. Four days later, the brother finds a pink slip in his office mailbox.

A sister overjoyed with the opportunity to get her dormmates to a Bible study, shares with "one too many" people. The resident adviser chastises her for "forcing her beliefs on others" and sets up a disciplinary meeting with the dorm director.

Another disciple, in his conviction to be righteous, informs workers who were smoking marijuana at the job site that if they don't stop, he will tell the foreman. The next day, he is shunned and works alone in silence.

You hang up the telephone. A sickening feeling overcomes you. Your mind sifts through the conversation wondering, "What did I do wrong?" as the words "I don't want to be a disciple anymore" echo painfully in your ears.

But we are called to get back up and run the race. In spite of opposition and disappointment, we must still reach out and make new friends. We must still be willing to risk our jobs and reputations to help others join us in the race. And we must still get up and continue the race even as we pass those who have looked back to the world and given up their crown.

Kip Keino persevered through physical pain to finish a race and receive a prize that was only temporal. We will also face suffering and pain of many kinds on our way to heaven. We must run with our hearts—big hearts full of love and full of faith.

INTO YOUR LIFE

1. What disappointment has been the most challenging for you to handle? Have you shared this with another disciple? What have you learned as you faced it?

2. What pain could you avoid if you just stopped trying to live as a disciple? Why are you willing to endure that pain and stay in the race?

3. Do you know of anyone who is thinking of giving up because they don't like the pain? What can you say to help them regain God's perspective?

4. Fear of persecution can keep us from being bold. When have you shrunk back this past week? Can you go back and take any of the opportunities that you missed?

5. When we are treated unjustly, we can become immobilized by bitterness. How can we keep from getting bitter? What attitude of heart did Jesus and the other disciples have when treated unjustly?

VICTORY OVER INTIMIDATION

Jesse Owens
· TRACK AND FIELD ·
United States

In 1931 when the 1936 Olympic Games were awarded to Berlin, few people had ever heard of Adolph Hitler. However, by the time of the event, the Third Reich was becoming a major force in the world, and Hitler used the Games to showcase his developing empire. His Nazi government was known for its racist views, and calls went out to move the Olympics to another site. Jewish communities in the U.S. and elsewhere urged that a boycott be staged, but the Games went on as planned without a single country refusing to participate.

Hitler spared no expense. He wanted the Berlin Olympics to be the most impressive ever held. A new 100,000 seat stadium was built that served as the centerpiece for a magnificent sports complex. For the first time, hundreds of runners teamed up to carry the Olympic torch from Greece to the site of the Games. Spiridon Louis, winner of the first Olympic marathon (see page 13) was brought in to present Hitler with an olive branch. The Germans had assured Olympic officials that there would be no discrimination against any athletes, but America's black team members were denounced by Nazi propaganda as "Black Auxiliaries."

Into this highly charged and intimidating atmosphere came African-American Jesse Owens. A year earlier in Columbus, Ohio, in one afternoon Jesse Owens had set five world records in five different events in what is still considered by many the greatest day ever in track and field. His long jump record stood for 25 years until broken by Bob Beamon (see page 73). But how would he perform under the pressure of Hitler and the Third Reich?

Owens first won the gold in the 100 meters, breaking the world record even on a wet track. The next morning he took another gold, breaking the Olympic record in the 200 meters. He nearly fouled out of the long jump competition, but with advice from the German jumper Luz Long, he qualified and went on to defeat Long for the gold. Thinking his time in the spotlight was over, Owens was unexpectedly pressed into service by his coach for the men's 4x100 relay team. The Americans set a world record, and Owens took home his fourth gold medal.

Lesser known African-Americans Archie Williams, John Woodruff and Cornelius Johnson also won gold in the 400 meters, 800 meters and high jump respectively. Hitler's "superior race" failed to intimidate these great athletes who competed with heart and soul.

Whatever happens, conduct yourselves in a manner worthy of the gospel of Christ. Then, whether I come and see you or only hear about you in my absence, I will know that you stand firm in one spirit, contending as one man for the faith of the gospel without being frightened in any way by those who oppose you. This is a sign to them that they will be destroyed, but that you will be saved—and that by God. For it has been granted to you on behalf of

Christ not only to believe on him, but also to suffer for him, since you are going through the same struggle you saw I had, and now hear that I still have.
PHILIPPIANS 1:27-30

When we studied to become disciples, most of us were taught very carefully that if we followed Jesus Christ we would be opposed. As we "counted the cost," we were warned that "everyone who wants to live a godly life in Christ Jesus will be persecuted" (2 Timothy 3:12). We needed to understand that there is simply no way to be the church of Jesus Christ and carry out the mission he has given without being criticized, condemned and strongly opposed.

Opposition can be intimidating. The word "intimidate" comes from Latin words which mean "to make intensively timid." Opposition can cause us to pull back. It can cause us to lose confidence. This is why better teams often will lose when playing before a boisterous crowd on their opponent's home court. Opposition can rattle us and cause us to lose composure. It can cause us to act unwisely.

Paul's message here to the Philippians was for them to stay united so they would not be frightened by those who opposed them. As we fight the good fight, we must overcome intimidation. We must be disciples in all situations no matter what others may say or what others may do. Paul says one of the keys to victory is staying very close to each other so that we do not fight separately but as though we were "one man."

Acts 4:23-31 shows another powerful weapon in our battle against intimidation. Not only were the disciples together and united, but they were *together and united in prayer*. Threatened by officials who wanted so much to intimidate them, they cried out to God in a prayer for boldness. Verse 31 describes the result: "After they prayed, the place where they were meeting was shaken. And they were all filled with the Holy Spirit and spoke the word of God boldly."

When marathon runners run through Boston, New York, L.A., Paris and other great cities, the crowds line the streets and cheer them on. When you run for Jesus Christ, fellow disciples will cheer you on, but a larger number may stand and boo. But with the help of God, the fellowship of the saints, and the courage of your own convictions, you can run through the glares and the stares and the jeers. Like Jesse Owens, you can be a beacon in the darkness.

INTO YOUR LIFE

1. List the two or three most intimidating situations you find yourself in as a disciple.

2. Try to describe what it is about these situations that intimidates you. What do you fear? What is the worst thing that can happen?

3. When you look at these things rationally, knowing that you serve Jesus Christ, the Lord of the Cosmos, how does it change your perspective?

4. How is being together and praying together with others helping you to overcome your fears? What changes need to be made to make the most of your fellowship with fellow believers?

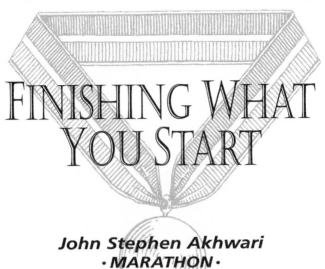

FINISHING WHAT YOU START

John Stephen Akhwari
· MARATHON ·
Tanzania

1968 was a year of worldwide political unrest. In America both Robert Kennedy and Martin Luther King Jr. had been gunned down. In Vietnam, war was being waged. The spirit of the times came also to Mexico, site of the Olympic Summer Games that year. First, the city officials of Mexico City were heavily criticized for building a costly stadium at a time when many of its people were living in poverty. Then demonstrations ensued, coming to a head on October 2, ten days before the start of the games. The Mexican army and protesters clashed, and when the riot had ended, 260 people's lives had also ended. More than 1200 others were injured.

Although the Games went on as planned, various incidents occurred which were detrimental to the spirit of unity that usually typifies the Games.

It is against this backdrop that the final Olympic event, the marathon, was held. The first runner to cross the finish line in this grueling test of endurance was Ethiopian runner Mamo Wolde. With his first place finish, Ethiopians had won three successive gold medals. Although Wolde was the champion, it was another African runner, John Stephen Akhwari from Tanzania, who truly ran the most glorious race that day. Although Akhwari did not win the gold or the silver or even the bronze, he won something more—the respect and honor of his fellowmen.

Most of the runners had finished the race and headed for the showers, and the crowd in the stadium had all but dispersed when John Stephen Akhwari came limping into the arena. He had one leg bandaged and seemed to be in terrible pain with each stride he took. The remaining few in the audience were at first stunned, then came to life and cheered Akhwari on as he slowly circled the track and crossed the finish line.

When Akhwari was asked why he didn't just drop out of the race, he replied, "I don't think you understand. My country did not send me to Mexico City to start the race. They sent me to finish the race." John Stephen Akhwari finished the race dead last. Yet it was his quiet example, his loyalty and courage that put him in the league of Olympic champions.

I have fought the good fight, I have finished the race, I have kept the faith.

2 TIMOTHY 4:7

Becoming an athlete requires a little bit of talent and a lot of drive. There's an expression something like "What he lacks in talent, he makes up for in enthusiasm." Many people who go out for sports have some level of talent, but a low level of enthusiasm. They never really develop the "killer instinct" that one really needs to become a successful athlete. They always teeter on the edge of "hanging it up" when the going gets tough.

As Christians, we have a strong adversary in Satan. He wounds us and injures us every chance he gets. He is after us and wants us to hang it up. He wants us to find ourselves in Akhwari's situation, struggling and in pain as we run our race. He wants us to teeter on the brink of quitting. He fills our heads with doubts and negative self-talk. He lies to us about ourselves and about the people in our lives. And he is relentless (1 Peter 5:8).

But we must decide, once and for all, that we did not enter the race just to start. We entered to finish, no matter the cost (Luke 9:23). And our race is daily. Each day we must arise and decide whether we're going to continue or whether we're going to step off the course. John Stephen Akhwari could have done that. He could have stepped off at any point and given up. Nobody would have faulted him. But he would have never heard those cheering voices or felt the pride of his countrymen. He could have stepped off into Olympic oblivion, but you are reading about him now just because of his decision to count the cost with every step his painful legs took. He is now a hero and a model of perseverance. He finished because he felt "sent" by his country.

John Stephen Akhwari did not get a medal or a crown that day. But he received something that could never be taken away from him: self-respect. A few unknown people cheering him on gave him the determination to finish the race.

We, too, have a great crowd of witnesses cheering us on (Hebrews 12:1). It's inspiring to think of Moses, Jonah, Gideon, Timothy, Peter, Paul and a host of other spiritual heroes pulling for us to finish. But more than anything else, we listen for the applause from the scarred hands of our Savior, cheering us towards the goal and waiting to catch us as we cross the finish line.

INTO YOUR LIFE

1. Do you feel sent? You may be running a steady race, but do you feel the sense of purpose behind it? Are you running aimlessly? Are you running to bring glory to the one who sent you?

2. Have you ever thought about getting out of the race and no longer being a disciple? What were you feeling? What were you thinking? Why will you never give in to those feelings or thoughts?

3. Read 2 Corinthians 5:14. In what ways does Christ's love *compel* you?

4. Imagine your entrance into heaven. Think about the heroes from the Bible and from the kingdom who will be there cheering for you at the finish. Feel the love from and for those people. In response, simply thank God.

5. Think of a brother or sister who is struggling to stay in the race. What can you do to cheer him or her on?

Week Four

PERSEVERANCE

NO MORE "I CAN'T"

Jim Abbott
· BASEBALL ·
United States

Baseball did not become an official medal sport in the Olympics until the Barcelona Games of 1992 when the Cubans took home the gold. However, in seven Olympiads before this, it had been a demonstration sport with some serious and sometimes dramatic competition. The rivalry between Cuba, Japan and the United States was particularly fierce.

In the Los Angeles Games of 1984, with the Cubans joining the Soviet boycott, the Japanese stunned the U.S. in the championship game—a huge upset in the minds of many. In Seoul in 1988, the U.S. team was eager to regain prominence. Once again it was the Japanese and the U.S. in the final game for the top prize.

The pitcher for the U.S. was the remarkable Jim Abbott, a native of Flint, Michigan, born 21 years earlier with no right hand (but to parents who told him he could accomplish anything he wanted to). In a game of skill that can be challenging enough for those with two hands, Jim Abbott had succeeded at every level with just one. He had pitched a no-hitter in his first Little League game. He had excelled in high school football, basketball and baseball and had gone on to star in the latter at the University of Michigan.

In the Olympic final, Abbott pitched well, and the U.S. team jumped out in front. In the eighth inning the Japanese team began a rally and closed the gap to 5-3. But then Abbott made a spectacular fielding play to throw out a Japanese runner and preserve the lead. An inning later Abbott finished a complete game and was surrounded by celebrating teammates. Later that year he was presented with the Sullivan Award as his country's most outstanding amateur athlete.

Jim Abbott was drafted by the California Angels and went on to a most successful career in major league baseball, pitching a coveted no-hitter on September 4, 1993, against the Cleveland Indians.

Hours spent in throwing a ball against a brick wall helped Abbott develop an incredible technique for catching the ball, shifting the glove to his right wrist and throwing with his left hand. Thousands who have seen him perform are amazed at his fluid motion. One of his former managers remarked, "Jim is the most *un*handicapped person I know."

With your help I can advance against a troop;
with my God I can scale a wall.

PSALM 18:29

I can do everything through him who gives me strength.

PHILIPPIANS 4:13

Some of life's challenges are easily overcome by the swift application of our own personal strengths. Others pinpoint our weaknesses, tempting us to listen to Satan as he whispers, "You don't measure up; so give up before you fail."

Jim Abbot was born with a handicap that would discour-

age most from even trying to play baseball. But his willingness to give his best and work hard has given us one of the
most heartwarming and glorious stories of overcoming in
Olympic history. Jim, without a doubt, went through many
very difficult times as he worked to do, with one arm, what
others find challenging with two. His heart was fixed on being a baseball player, though, and he did whatever was needed
to be the best he could be. Through his failures he did not
give up, but tried variations until he succeeded. This enabled him to develop strengths and abilities most people never
know they have.

As we strive to become like Jesus, we must apply Jim's
example to our own spiritual lives. One of Satan's most powerful weapons is to show us our weakness and then con-
vince us we cannot change or grow. God's heart is that we
willingly apply the talents and abilities *we have* been given by
him. As we do this, we too, will face those times when we
wonder if we can do it. But failures must never be seen as
defeats. They only indicate that God desires for us to take a
different route to the goal.

Imagine the many frustrations Jim must have experienced
until he finally developed the technique which now causes
people to marvel. How many times did he say, "That didn't
work, I need to try a different way"? The one thing Jim never
said was "I can't; so I'm going to quit trying."

The statement, "I can't," is a faithless statement that de-
nies the promises of God. As disciples, we have seen God
do incredible things in our lives, yet most of us have some
area that is stubbornly resistant to change. Jim had no guar-
antee that he could succeed, only determination to pursue
his goal. As disciples, though, we have God's Holy Spirit
that ensures us the victory. Do not allow weakness and failure to cause you to quit. Dig deeper and search for another
way. Let your weakness be the catalyst to finding your greatest strength. Persevere, and you will understand more deeply
the incredible love, power and grace of our God.

INTO YOUR LIFE

1. What do you like about Jim Abbott's story?

2. What is your "handicap"? What is something that is true of you that could be seen as a major obstacle to spiritual success?

3. Describe your present attitude toward this "handicap."

4. In a conversation with Jesus, what things do you think he would say to you about your challenge in this area?

5. When you encounter failure, what do you tend to do next? How can you apply the lesson from Jim Abbott to some area of failure you have experienced?

OVERCOMING THE SADNESS

Oksana Baiul
· FIGURE SKATING ·
Ukraine

The people of the Ukraine have had their share of misfortune throughout history. In the 13th century they were conquered by the Mongolians and Ghengis Khan. The region was ruled by other outsiders from the 14th to 17th centuries, and then came under Russian control late in the 18th century. During World War II the Ukraine was devastated by German occupation for three years. Then in 1986 came Chernobyl and the worst nuclear power accident in history—an incident that continues to claim lives today.

Yet, the Ukrainians are a resilient and hopeful people. In 1991 the Ukraine was established as a separate republic, and three years later they sent a young figure skater to Lillehammer, Norway, with a chance to be the first Olympic winner for their new sovereign state.

Like the country she represented, young Oksana Baiul had a sad history. As a child, her father had abandoned her. Then when she was only thirteen, Baiul's mother died from cancer. After her death Oksana moved in with her grandparents, but shortly afterwards, they too died. A year later her coach, one of the few lasting and stable influences in her life, moved away to Canada. Things must have seemed very bleak for this vulnerable teenager.

It was at this point that Galina Zmievskaya would come into Baiul's life. Zmievskaya was the coach and mother-in-law of Olympic gold medalist Victor Petrenko. She was also a woman with a big heart. When Petrenko asked her if she would consider coaching Baiul, she agreed not only to coach her, but wanted Baiul to live with her and be part of her family as well.

Under Zmievskaya's direction, Baiul made the Olympic figure skating finals. The battle for the gold medal came down to a test between only two—Baiul and American Nancy Kerrigan. When the night was over, only one tenth of a point would separate them, yet Baiul would win.

It was an emotional moment for Oksana, who expressed her thankfulness to her new coach and family, "To achieve great things in life, with the help of others, one can overcome the sadness of the past." It was surely a time of joy for both Oksana Baiul and for the Ukraine.

My eyes fail from weeping,
*   I am in torment within,*
my heart is poured out on the ground
*   because my people are destroyed,*
because children and infants faint
*   in the streets of the city.*
                                    LAMENTATIONS 2:11

Because of the LORD's great love we are not
*   consumed,*
*   for his compassions never fail.*
They are new every morning;
*   great is your faithfulness.*

I say to myself, "The Lord is my portion;
therefore I will wait for him."
LAMENTATIONS 3:22-24

"The sadness of the past." A phrase that describes what is felt in so many people's lives. Jeremiah, as he penned the words above from Lamentations 2, was among a people who needed to overcome the sadness and tragedy of the past. Their once great nation had been left in ruins. Their people had seen starvation, sickness and death. Few were left with any hope.

Many people get stuck in the sadness and the "badness" of the past and never emerge from it. Some people look back on homes where there was physical, emotional and sexual abuse, and some of these people never heal. Some people look back on a past when their tribe, their race, their ethnic group or their religious group was discriminated against, and they stay bitter about those experiences all their lives.

Some people look back on broken dreams and devastated expectations, and they never get beyond their resentment or their cynicism. They think about the father they never had, the family they never had, the marriage they never had, the children they never had. Or they think about the father they *did have* and the family they *did have* and the marriage (and then divorce) they *did have* and how difficult all those were. Day after day, year after year, they carry all of their hurts with them in a big bag, as it were, across their backs. And then, tragically, they pass all this sadness, hurt, pain or anger on to another generation.

Life can be tough. The race can be long and hard. The disappointments can be painful. But no matter what the past has been like, we must go on to the faith Jeremiah went on to express: "Because of the Lord's great love we are *not consumed*, for his compassions never fail" (Lamentations 3:22, emphasis added).

The sadness or hurt of the past does not have to consume us. God can heal us if we want to get well. God can send "Galinas" into our lives to love us and give us encouragement. He can give us relationships that renew our hearts. We may never forget the past and its pains, but we can overcome the past and its distress.

God's compassions are "new every morning." But they are not only there daily; they are big enough to overshadow any sadness. With the help of God and with the mercy of God applied to our lives, there is no pain of the past that cannot be overcome. To allow the darkness of the past to keep us from doing the right thing now is to allow our enemy to have victories he should not and must not have. *Whatever* has happened, we can rise again and joyfully go on to things that are good and right.

INTO YOUR LIFE

1. What is there in your past that could be "baggage," a weight that you have trouble getting rid of?

2. How has your faith and your walk with God helped you to deal with this challenge?

3. Is there anything in the past that you have not come to terms with and allowed God to take off you? Who are you willing to talk to about this? When will you do it?

4. Is there anything you would be willing to do for God if you could just resolve some things from your past? Will you share this with someone this week?

5. What is true about your faith that makes it possible for pain in the past to be completely overcome by joy?

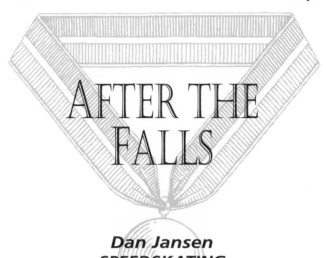

AFTER THE FALLS

Dan Jansen
· SPEEDSKATING ·
United States

In 1984 at the age of eighteen, Dan Jansen entered his first Olympic final—the 500-meter speed-skating race, and just missed a bronze medal. Not discouraged by his first appearance, he returned in 1990 to Calgary as the favorite to win the gold medal in the 500 meters as well as the 1,000 meters.

Early in the day of the 500-meter finals, Dan received the news that his sister, Jane, who had been fighting leukemia, had died. Predictably distraught, Dan was assured by his family that Jane would want him to race, and he took his place in the field. But less than 100-meters around the track he lost his balance and fell. His countrymen grieved with him. He picked himself up, and four days later was setting the pace in the 1,000-meters—surely headed for his first gold medal. With only one lap to go, Jansen once again lost his footing and was out of the race. He lost the gold, but more importantly, he had lost his sister, and he hurried home from Calgary to be with his family.

Determined to win, he returned four years later in 1992 to the Games held in Albertville. As usual Jansen was predicted to medal, but he placed fourth in the 500-meters and finished the 1,000-meter race far behind the winners. Again Jansen had failed to perform under pressure.

Two years later in 1994, the winter games would be held in Lillehammer. (The Olympic committee agreed to change the cycle of the Winter Games.) Dan Jansen was given one last shot. He knew that this would be his last chance to compete. In the 500-meter race, Jansen looked like a surefire winner. His wife and new daughter, named Jane after his sister, were in the stands cheering him on. Then into the last turn of the race, it happened: He fell. The pain of Calgary returned. As he fell, so did his spirit and his belief that he could ever win.

Four days later Dan Jansen lined up for the last Olympic race of his career: the 1,000 meters. He was a beaten man, he recalled later. He had lost his hope of winning, but he had not lost his courage to fight. He then proceeded to give the greatest performance of his career, and although he slipped on one turn, he held on to win the Olympic gold medal. Dan Jansen proved that forgetting what's behind and pressing on towards the goal is what makes a real champion.

...for though a righteous man falls seven times,
*   he rises again,*
but the wicked are brought down by calamity.
                    PROVERBS 24:16

If you have ever watched a young child determined to learn to ice skate, you have probably learned a lot about perseverance. Fall after fall, they have the resiliency to get back up and keep on improving. Holding in front of their minds the desire to please their parents and the image of the glorious figure skaters they have seen on TV, they press on toward their goal of greatness. The improvement is slow and the falls are many, but they maintain their drive to succeed.

Sounds a lot like the Christian walk. There are many falls. Sometimes it's hard to get back up. Dan Jansen surely felt that. Lying on the ice after his fall, particularly the last one, he must have felt agonizing regret.

Sometimes when we fall, we lie down longer than we should, pondering the circumstances. *Why has this happened to me? I don't deserve this! I thought you loved me, God. I should not even have tried. I knew I'd never make it.* The negative self-talk begins to flow like lava. What we need when we're lying there on the ice is the warm glow of the Spirit's fire to remind us of who we really are.

There once was an apostle named Peter who had his share of falls. "'Are you so dull?' asked Jesus" (Matthew 15:16). That was at least a minor slip. Then, "Get behind me, Satan!" (Matthew 16:23). Ouch! That one hurt a bit more. Finally, the infamous rooster (Matthew 26:75). That one broke him. He must have "laid on the ice" for a while on that one, weeping until he could weep no longer. But we know that the Spirit's power came and caused him to arise in such a bold way that he set forth to turn the world upside down.

Dan Jansen overcame his falls and went on to be a winner. He got a medal of gold hung around his neck and received commercial endorsements and adulation from the world. Peter overcame his falls and was given the greatest endorsement of all: He was chosen as the spokesman of God. After Jesus' ascension, Peter was the first to tell people how they could be forgiven of their sins and enter the kingdom of God. Because he was willing to get back up, he was blessed with a victor's crown and a reward that will last forever (1 Corinthians 9:25).

INTO YOUR LIFE

1. In your walk with God, in which areas do you most often fall? What can you do to lessen the number of times you fall?

2. Have you been through a particularly difficult challenge lately? How did you respond? Did you "lie on the ice" for a long time, or did you get up and keep going?

3. When you fall, what kind of self-talk do you engage in? Do you give in to negative, faithless thinking, or do you "take captive every thought"? (See 2 Corinthians 10:5.)

4. What words do you think God most wants you to hear from him when you fall?

The Interests of Others

Lawrence Lemieux
• BOARDSAILING •
Canada

Lawrence Lemieux is a hero with heart. In the 1988 Olympic Games, he was competing in the fifth race of a seven-race event. As part of the Finn class, he sailed solo in a centerboard dinghy. The conditions were not the best for sailing that day. Winds of 15 knots are acceptable, but winds were gusting up to 35 knots.

Halfway through the course, Lemieux noticed that a boat in a nearby 470 race had capsized. One of the two Singapore crew members, Joseph Chan, had injured his back in the accident. Not only was Chan stranded 25 feet away from his boat, but he was being carried away by a fast-moving current. His partner, Shaw Her Siew, was clinging to the overturned boat with no chance of righting it himself.

Sailing in second place at the time, Lemieux knew he had a good chance of receiving a medal in the overall competition. But as soon as he assessed the danger of the situation, he took immediate action. He pulled out of his race and maneuvered into position to rescue Chan. The sailor was too injured and exhausted to pull himself into the boat.

Lemieux dragged him aboard, taking the risk of capsizing his own boat. Then he repeated the rescue with Siew.

Waiting with the two wet, but grateful, men for the patrol boat to reach him, Lemieux knew there was no chance of his gaining lost ground (or wind). After transferring the two, he did rejoin the race, finishing 22nd out of 32.

When news of the unselfish rescue reached the ears of the jury of the International Yacht Racing Union, they voted unanimously to award Lemieux a second-place finish in the fifth race. Not one of the other contestants questioned the decision. It is highly likely, though, that many of them questioned their own hearts.

Although the Canadian sailor did not win a medal in the seven-race competition, he did win the respect and appreciation of all who heard the story. At the medal awards ceremony, the president of the International Olympic Committee honored this good Samaritan for his unselfish actions: "By your sportsmanship, self-sacrifice and courage, you embody all that is right with the Olympic ideal."

Lemieux did not return to Canada with a medal around his neck, but he did return a winner.

Each of you should look not only to your own interests, but also to the interests of others.
PHILIPPIANS 2:4

When the competitive juices are flowing, when our performance is being compared to that of others, when we have a chance to be Number 1, the most natural thing is to ask "How does this affect me? What can I do to make sure I come out on top, that I look good, that I get what I have worked so hard to get?" So natural is our tendency toward self-centeredness that it takes an act of the will, or at least a diligently trained character, to focus on the interests of others.

Lawrence Lemieux performed an act of self-denial. When asked about his choice, he simply reminded reporters of what would have happened if he had not gone after Chan. Surely his conscience would have plagued him if he had stayed in the race and Chan had needlessly died. But Jesus calls us not just to perform rare self-sacrificing acts. He calls us to die daily to ourselves, to live every day seeking to please God and to serve others. In short, he calls us to take on his heart and his attitude:

> *Who, being in very nature God,*
> > *did not consider equality with God something*
> > > *to be grasped,*
> *but made himself nothing,*
> > *taking the very nature of a servant,*
> > *being made in human likeness.*
> *And being found in appearance as a man,*
> > *he humbled himself*
> > *and became obedient to death—even death*
> > > *on a cross! (Philippians 2:6-8).*

In a race he had already won, Jesus left his "position" to come rescue us. He did more than just perform acts of self-denial; he totally denied himself ("made himself nothing," NIV; "emptied himself," RSV, Philippians 2:6). Paul says that "each of us should please his neighbor for his good, to build him up. For even Christ did not please himself" (Romans 15:2-3). In fact, he denied himself all the way to a cross.

In Philippians 2 Paul urges the disciples to have the same radical concern for each other that Jesus has for each of them. He calls them not to think naturally, but to think spiritually. He calls them to pull out of a race that is going well for them, and help someone who has capsized in their own race. This happens when we see someone being made fun of, and we befriend them; when we don't get our own work done in order to help a distraught coworker; when we lose our sleep

THE HEART OF A CHAMPION

to help someone who needs time to talk through a hurt; when we pour ourselves into helping someone become a Christian even though someone else may get the credit.

When we make these choices of the heart, we probably will get no medals. Most will never even notice our decision to sacrifice. But "Heaven's Committee" will notice and will honor us as Jesus was honored:

> *Therefore God exalted him to the highest place and gave him the name that is above every name (Philippians 2:9).*

INTO YOUR LIFE

1. What would you have felt in Lawrence Lemieux's situation? How could he have rationalized staying in his own race?

2. In what ways have you been called to "leave your race" to help someone else? When you did it, what convinced you that you had done the right thing?

3. When you daily live to meet the needs of others, do you believe that God will meet your needs? (See Philippians 4:19.) How has he proven this to you in the past?

4. Why are you so convinced that the way to find your life is to lose it?

A WINNING WIND

Åsa Linares
· BOARDSAILING/PARALYMPICS ·
Sweden/Kingdom of God

Sailing is a physically and mentally demanding sport. Working in tandem with nature can be more of a challenge than simply working in tandem with teammates. Of course, team sailing means coordinating both of these aspects.

Can you imagine being a sailor and missing one arm? How about missing one arm and one leg below the knee?

Åsa Linares does not have to imagine either: She lives with both every day of her life. Åsa's birth defect was caused because her mother took the prescription drug thalidomide during pregnancy. After she had an allergic reaction to an artificial leg she wore for years, she was forced to use a wheelchair. It was eight long years before she could once again walk with the aid of a new artificial leg. During this difficult time of transition, she began to seek God. She was found by him and *baptized as a disciple of Jesus* on January 9, 1987, in the church in Stockholm.

Åsa was not going to let dual disabilities stop her or even slow her down. After becoming a disciple, she sought a way to overcome her limitations. Before being in the wheelchair, she had competed in both water skiing and downhill skiing. Unable to stand and compete, she took up sailing. What courage! What determination! What faith!

Forming a team with two other disabled sailors, she sailed to fourth place for Sweden in the 1993 First World Championships of Disabled Sailing. In a demonstration of tenacity and discipline, she and her teammates worked their way to a second place ranking in 1994 in the same event. The next year, her team placed third in the European Championship.

Perhaps Åsa's most amazing accomplishment, though, is placing third in a different, more demanding race: a mixed class competition of disabled and non-disabled women and men sailing in one-person boats. In this competition, she had no one to help her—no one, that is, except the one who walked on the water through which she sails.

At the writing of this book, Åsa is preparing for the 1996 pre-Paralympic trials in St. Petersburg, Florida. She hopes to be selected as part of the team representing Sweden.

Constantly aware of God as she is surrounded by his creation, she relies on him when she races. Since sailing on a competitive level, she has seen her faith develop and strengthen. She says, "When I think I am doing poorly, God shows himself at the last minute by granting a winning wind—it never fails!"

A woman who could have tried to justify bitterness for a "bum rap" in life, grows daily in her thankfulness to a God who loves and supports her as she goes for Olympic gold.

At my first defense, no one came to my support, but everyone deserted me. May it not be held against them. But the Lord stood at my side and gave me strength, so that through me the message might be fully proclaimed and all the Gentiles might hear it.

2 TIMOTHY 4:16-17

God is clear in the New Testament that he wants his people to support each other. He wants us to be there for each other, to share strength and courage with each other. But for each of us, just as for Paul, there are times when no other disciples are there. Have you ever been struggling with something, knowing you need input from someone? Or maybe you are hurting about something and need to share your load with someone who cares? You call everybody you know and get either a busy signal or "Please leave your message at the tone..." You hang up the phone, feeling empty and alone. You sigh. Then comes the time of character-testing: *Who will I talk to? Who will help me? Who will care about what is happening to me?* Do you then catch yourself and say, "Oh, yeah. The friend who sticks closer than a brother. Jesus. Oh, yeah. God, my Father"?

When this happens, we realize that we cannot trust primarily in each other. Not only can we not always *locate* each other, but "each other" can die or move or even fall away. Many times God placed a loyal friend with Paul for encouragement (Colossians 4:11; Romans 16:3, 13). But at other times God allowed Paul to go through the trials without a trusted brother by his side (see 2 Timothy 4 above). In both situations God was at work. Working through people at one time and working through reliance on him alone at another.

As our sister Åsa sails, she has come to know the power and encouragement of working with a team, of synchronizing and coordinating thoughts and movements. She has also experienced the challenge and thrill of being out on the water with only her boat and her God.

However you may be "sailing" at any given point, alone or with a team, remember that God is your source and your navigator. With his help, you won't lose your direction, and you won't lose the race. You will become one with the "winning wind."

INTO YOUR LIFE

1. Can you think of a time that you felt the need to talk with someone, but no one was available? Did you get frustrated, or did you turn back to God? How do you keep the balance of relying on others but not forgetting to rely on God?

2. Do you tend to be open or aloof with other Christians? Do you share your struggles and ask for help? Do you share your joys and feel close to others? Or do you tend to keep things to yourself?

3. Do you tend to "sail" better alone or with a team? What do you need to learn in both situations?

4. How does it cause you to feel when you realize that God is with you wherever you go, whatever you do? How deep is your conviction on this point?

DOWN BUT NOT OUT

Luisito Espinosa
· BOXER ·
Philippines/Kingdom of God

There is something about boxing that stirs the emotions. The elements tend to sweep one along: the challenge, the drama, the guts and the excitement. One on one, face to face, toe to toe. Each opponent seeking to outwit, outmaneuver, overpower or master the other.

A true-life, modern hero of the boxing ring began his career in the Philippines, and then was reborn there both spiritually and athletically. It's not Philadelphia's "Rocky Balboa," but Manila's Luisito ("Louie") Espinosa, a disciple of Jesus Christ. As this book goes to press, he is the reigning WBC Featherweight Champion of the World. Louie captured the hearts and minds of the Philippine nation, appearing on the front page of every major newspaper in the country, speaking on many television and radio shows, and of course, shaking hands with the President.

Why such an impact? Luisito was born in Tondo, one of the poorest sections of Manila—a stone's throw from the infamous Smokey Mountain. From all angles, his life was a challenge. His natural mother died when he was seven years old, and he grew up in a family consisting of nine brothers and five sisters.

Louie's father, once a boxing champion himself, worked as a personal cook in the Malacanang Palace, serving the late President, Ferdinand Marcos. As a poor boy living in the outskirts of the palace compound, Louie was enamored by his father's boxing trophies, and often went to bed hugging his father's boxing gloves instead of the usual "teddy bear." Since he couldn't send Louie to school, Egnedio taught his son the only thing he knew how to do—box in the ring. As he trained in the palace grounds, Louie remembered once saying to former-President Marcos, "Someday, you will watch me on TV, winning a championship!" to which Marcos replied, "How can that be? You're too skinny!" With perseverance Louie pushed on toward an impossible dream.

In July 1989, during one of the largest earthquakes in Philippine history (8.0 on the Richter Scale), Louie won the WBA Bantamweight Championship in Thailand, thus earning him the nickname "Lindol" or "Earthquake." The glory of that championship, however, was quickly lost, as Louie was defeated in his first defense in Mexico City that same year. Down and distraught, Louie caused many to wonder if his career was over.

In November of 1993, a group of disciples who were out for an early morning quiet time recognized Louie and his wife, Maricherie. A simple invitation, coupled with a lot of heart and perseverance by the Christians resulted in a Bible study that would change Louie's heart, life and destiny forever. Louie and Maricherie were baptized into Christ in just one week. With a new Lord, a new life, and a new wave of inspiration, Louie overcame fears and failures and hungrily eyed a comeback.

Louie not only trained physically, he trained harder spiritually. Though many temptations to compromise abounded (for no other boxer had the challenge of juggling a rigorous training schedule with the demands of a disciple's ministry),

Louie kept his treasure, and his heart, firmly in heaven. Louie held fast to his commitment to Jesus, clinging to the simple faith that if one puts God first, victory will come according to his will.

In December 1995 after overcoming many trials both physically and spiritually, Louie won the WBC Featherweight crown in a convincing 10-round decision in Tokyo. Later he retained his title with a victory over a top contender in Mexico City (all the while wearing shorts decorated with the logo from the Metro Manila Arts/Media/Sports ministry). Louie was in the ring wanting not his own glory, but God's.

What's in the future for the champ? Louie just wants God's will. Ministry? Working with the poor? Whatever pleases God. This poor boy from Tondo has learned to put his confidence in the right trainer.

For our struggle is not against flesh and blood, but against the rulers, against the authorities, against the powers of this dark world and against the spiritual forces of evil in the heavenly realms.

EPHESIANS 6:12

Life in Christ is no game. It is a serious fight. Luisito Espinosa will tell you he has learned that the real opponent is not another boxer in shorts and gloves. The real opponent is an unseen spiritual enemy who, nevertheless, is resilient and relentless. Louie's experiences in the boxing ring have certainly had value, making him more aware than ever of how to win the spiritual battle. He is now convinced that the real glory is found not in landing a punch on a man, but in dealing Satan a crushing blow. To this end he trains and prays. All who want to be disciples must join him.

In our own spiritual battles, we may, like Louie, win a victory over our opponent and then later be disappointed with a defeat. At that point the enemy becomes the ultimate "trash talker," taunting us, ridiculing us, demeaning us, laughing at us. He wants us to believe our success against him was a fluke and that our faith will fail. But, like Louie, we must learn that with God's power we can make as many comebacks as we need to make. Knocked down does not mean knocked out.

We can expect our fight against Satan to be a tough one. We can expect from him some fancy footwork, some low blows and some punishing body punches. But whatever the score at the end of Round 1, or Round 7, or Round 14, we must be confident that "...in all these things we are more than conquerors through him who loved us" (Romans 8:37). If we stay "strong in the Lord and in his mighty power" (Ephesians 6:10) we cannot lose. Just ask Louie.

INTO YOUR LIFE

1. What is your biggest fight with Satan? What "blows" is he delivering?

2. Looking at the last two weeks of your life, how would the judges score your fight with the enemy? Where did he score his points? Where did you score yours? Who is ahead?

3. How confident are you that God's power will always be sufficient to help you conquer your opponent? What kind of study helps your confidence to grow? What kinds of prayers help your confidence to grow? What kind of fellowship helps your confidence to grow?

4. What three principles would you give to a "young fighter" about how to go into the ring with Satan and come out a winner?

NEVER QUIT

Glenn Cunningham
· TRACK ·
United States

It was February 1916. Seven-year-old Glenn Cunningham and two brothers and a sister walked against the strong cold wind blowing across the Kansas prairie. The two-mile walk from their home to their school left them exhausted. Arriving at the small building before anyone else, the three boys entered through a side entrance while their sister played outside. Glenn's older brother Floyd decided to start the fire in the potbellied stove while Glenn and Raymond played tick-tack-toe.

When Floyd poured liquid over the coals from a can that usually held kerosene, there was a huge explosion that knocked Glenn against the wall. The can, carelessly left the night before by a community club, contained gasoline, not kerosene, and embers from the previous fire were still smoldering. The result was catastrophic. Immediately Floyd's clothes were in flames and so were Glenn's. The smell of burning flesh made both boys vomit. The three brothers finally escaped from the building now engulfed in flames and somehow ran and walked the two miles back to their home.

After lingering with a badly burned body for weeks, Floyd finally died. Glenn would live, but the doctors said it was unlikely that he would walk again, so severe were the burns on his legs.

He remembers fighting back the tears and resolving in his heart that he would not give up. The Cunningham family motto had always been "Never quit." Encouraged by the words of his father, he was not only convinced that he would not only walk again but run as well.

With many telling him he couldn't do it and with every effort to improve bringing intense pain, young Glenn decided deep in the core of his being that he would give his all. Slowly he made progress. He walked again, and he ran again. And he ran and ran and ran. Almost always in pain, he still ran. Amazingly, he won an athletic scholarship and ran on the track team for the University of Kansas. The legs never stopped aching, but Glenn never stopped running. In 1932 he set a new collegiate record in the mile run and made the Olympic team. The day of the 1500-meter competition he was stricken with an infected tonsil, and in his weakened condition could only finish fourth.

In the years between the L.A. Olympics and the '36 Games in Berlin, Cunningham set the world indoor record for the mile at Madison Square Garden and the world outdoor record in a meet at Princeton. Before a crowd of 100,000 in the Berlin Olympic stadium in 1936, he went for a gold medal. Halfway through the race, the blinding pain in his legs was so intense he nearly fell, but with only a few meters to go he was still in the lead. At the last moment he was passed by Jack Lovelock of New Zealand. Cunningham took home the silver medal, but what an accomplishment that was! The boy who was not supposed to walk had said to himself, "Never quit," and he ran with the greatest in the world.

Let us not become weary in doing good, for at the proper time we will reap a harvest if we do not give up.

Never quit. What a great motto! What power it brings to our lives when there is a conviction deep within that says "I will never quit." Stop for a moment and just say the words out loud. Those words that Glenn Cunningham's father planted in his children may have been the difference between a life of victory and wasted years of self-pity.

When we leave the back door open, when we think we can always bail out if the going gets too tough, we have already set ourselves up for defeat. But when we decide that we will not give up, the power of perseverance that will not be denied begins to grow within us.

Listen to the disciple of Jesus who has this attitude burning in his or her soul:

I may get hit. I may get knocked down. I may feel pain. I may feel fatigue, but I will never quit.

I may sin. I may fail. I may disappoint myself or others, but I will keep righteousness as my goal, and I will never quit.

I will seek the lost as long as there is breath in my body. I may be rejected. I may be hurt. My heart may be broken, but I will never quit.

I may be persecuted, opposed, ridiculed, slandered or ignored because of my faith, but I will never quit.

I will love the church and seek to make her great and strong. Difficulties may come. Satan may win some victories, but I will never quit.

I will love my brothers and sisters. They will not always meet my expectations. They may need my forgiveness and I may need theirs. We may have to work long and hard to make our relationships great, but I will never quit.

Life may surprise me with illness, with death, with injury, with depression. I may reel and stagger, but I will never quit.

My arms may weaken. My legs may ache and burn when I run. My eyes may grow dim, but I will never quit.

The lion may roar. My enemies may shout. The world may shake. The storms may come. The floods may rise, but I will never quit.

I am a disciple of Jesus Christ, and I will be a disciple of Jesus as long as I live. I will fight the good fight of faith until I have nothing left. I will run until I have finished the race. I will never ever quit.

INTO YOUR LIFE

1. Have you adopted a "never quit" attitude with regard to the Christian race?

2. If you said yes, why have you made this decision? If you said, no, what keeps you from declaring this to be your attitude?

3. Say the words aloud: *I will never quit.* Say them again. How do you feel when you make that statement? Can you sense the power that these words produce?

4. Jesus never quit. He went all the way to "It is finished." How will he help you go all the way to the finish?

5. This week get with someone who knows you well. Look them in the eye and say, "Whatever happens, I will never quit."

BIBLIOGRAPHY

Associated Press, The. *The Olympics at 100: A Celebration in Pictures.* Text by Larry Siddons. New York: Macmillan, 1995.

Cunningham, Glenn. *Never Quit.* Lincoln, Virginia: Chosen Books, 1981.

Discovery Channel Multimedia, The. *Olympic Gold: A 100-Year History of the Summer Olympic Games.* S.E.A Multimedia Ltd., 1995. CD-ROM Windows.

Franklin, Marie. "Racing Toward a College Degree, Too." *The Boston Sunday Globe*, April 14, 1991.

Greenspan, Bud. *100 Greatest Moments in Olympic History.* Los Angeles: General Publishing Group, Inc., 1995.

Madden, Michael. "Hoyt's Illustrate a Real Triumph of Human Spirit." *The Boston Globe*, July 17, 1990.

Powers, John. "Marathoning's Doubles Team." *The Boston Globe*, April 16, 1990.

Shepherd, Preston. "A Crown That Will Last." *L.A. Story*, Volume 3, Issue 5, March 31, 1996.

The United States Olympic Committee. *The Olympic Factbook: A Spectator's Guide to the Summer Games.* Edited by Rebecca Nelson and Marie J. MacNee. Detroit: Visible Ink Press, 1996.

Wallechinsky, David. *The Complete Book of the Olympics.* Boston: Little Brown and Company, 1992.

The Daily Power Series
Series Editors: Thomas and Sheila Jones

Thirty Days at the Foot of the Cross
A study of the central issue of Christianity

First...the Kingdom
A study of the Sermon on the Mount

The Mission
The inspiring task of the church in every generation

Teach Us to Pray
A study of the most vital of all spiritual disciplines

To Live Is Christ
An interactive study of the Letter to the Philippians

Glory in the Church
God's plan to shine through his church

The Victory of Surrender
An in-depth study of a powerful biblical concept
(workbook and tapes also available)
by Gordon Ferguson

The Fine Art of Hospitality
edited by Sheila Jones
The Fine Art of Hospitality Handbook
edited by Sheila Jones and Betty Dyson
(two-volume set)

Life to the Full
A study of the writings of James, Peter, John and Jude
by Douglas Jacoby

True and Reasonable
Evidences for God in a skeptical world
by Douglas Jacoby

Raising Awesome Kids in Troubled Times
by Sam and Geri Laing

Let It Shine: A Devotional Book for Teens
edited by Thomas and Sheila Jones

Mind Change: The Overcomer's Handbook
by Thomas A. Jones

She Shall Be Called Woman
Volume I: Old Testament Women
edited by Sheila Jones and Linda Brumley

She Shall Be Called Woman
Volume II: New Testament Women
edited by Sheila Jones and Linda Brumley

The Disciple's Wedding
by Nancy Orr with Kay McKean

The Unveiling
Exploring the Nature of God
by Curt Simmons

For information about ordering these
and many other resources from DPI, call
1-800-727-8273
or from outside the U.S.
617-938-7396
or write to
DPI, One Merrill Street, Woburn, MA 01801-4629